101 COOL BUILDINGS

the best of New York City architecture 1999-2009

Richard McMillan

Copyright 2009 Richard McMillan

All rights reserved. No part of this publication may be reproduced or transmitted in any form or by any means, electronic or mechanical, including photocopying, recording, or by any information storage and retrieval system, without prior permission in writing from the copyright holder, except in the case of brief quotations embodied in critical articles and reviews.

Cover and interior design: Pollyn C. Horvath

ISBN:1-4392-4316-6

Acknowledgements

Thank you to New York City for being my home for the last ten years.
It hasn't always been easy, but it's definitely been good.

Thank you to the architects who generously took time to share information and stories about these great buildings.

Thank you to Pollyn Horvath of Pollyn Design Studio, who brought the book visually to life.

And thank you to Pamela Cameron and Ivy Liu for inspiration and encouragement.

Contents

Introduction

This is a guidebook for visitors and residents who are interested in experiencing New York City's most exciting new architecture. Rest assured: there is a great deal to see! In the last ten years New York has once more embraced the conviction that daring architectural design has an important place in urban life. This is a welcome change in attitude from the emphasis on preservation which prevailed through much of the 1990s, when focus on restoring revered city landmarks (such as the Statue of Liberty, the New York Public Library Building, and Grand Central Terminal) stole the limelight from designers and clients who wanted to push the architectural envelope.

The renewed acceptance of groundbreaking design has been spurred in part by the success of such high-profile architects as Frank Gehry, Santiago Calatrava and Richard Meier, whose recent projects have instantly become international tourist destinations. Happily, all of these architects are now working on projects in New York, as is a dazzling lineup of local, national and international talent. The result is that a proliferation of sophisticated new projects is now scattered throughout the city.

The 101 projects here represent a great deal of work by a great many people. As an architect myself, I can appreciate the tears and sweat which go into realizing a dream. My hope is that this guide proves interesting and useful to anyone who has an interest in New York City and in exciting new architecture. The buildings here should serve not only as amenities to their neighbors and (especially) to their users, but as inspiration to those who will create the next generation of new construction in the city. Here's looking forward to the next ten years!

Richard McMillan
Spring 2009

1

Staten Island Whitehall Ferry Terminal
1 South Street (at Whitehall St.)
Frederic Schwartz Architects
TAMS Consultants
2005

Replacement of the previous building, completed in the 1950s and fire-damaged in 1991, took fourteen years and three mayors. Design competition winners Robert Venturi and Denise Scott-Brown ended their involvement after the city demanded revisions to their successful entry (a 120-foot clock tower which was to be the centerpiece of the design was eliminated). Fred Schwartz soldiered on as design architect, with TAMS Consultants as architect of record. The need for two out of the three slips to remain open at all times led to the preparation of nearly 100 sheets of elaborate construction phasing plans.

The irregularly-shaped building boasts full-height fenestration and a sweeping entry canopy, whose supergraphic lettering is reinterpreted inside as oversized digital signage. Expansive terraces at the second level take full advantage of the stunning Lower Manhattan views. The floor plan was driven by requirements for accommodating massive passenger circulation (as many as 6,000 people board or disembark at one time). The recent completion of the subway terminal below the adjacent Peter Minuit Plaza stirs hope that the building will soon embrace a complementary outdoor space.

to Whitehall St.

1 to South Ferry

2

Pier 11
Wall Street and South Street
Smith-Miller + Hawkinson Architects
2000

In keeping with the simple program—a waiting area for ferry passengers—the architects established a simple architectonic concept: a shed roof defines the envelope of the building, and the space underneath is filled with a changeable composition of solids and voids. Building elements are a combination of transparent and opaque forms, including a moveable south wall which allows the interior waiting area to be open in good weather.

The designers chose a prosaic but appealing materials palette (painted steel, corrugated metal, terne shingles, anodized curtain wall, and stainless steel), which is tailored to the nautical setting. At the interior waiting area, blonde wood is introduced to provide visual warmth. The machine room, thrust out from the building and enclosed in glass, is typical of the building's celebration of utilitarian features. Overall, this is a basic architectural idea executed with style and elegance.

2 3 4 5 to Wall St.

3

114-116 Hudson Street Condominiums
114-116 Hudson Street (at Moore St.)
BKSK Architects LLP
2005

This project renovated a five-story nineteenth-century building and constructed a new seven-story building next door. The new building extends over the existing to create one structure of a uniform height, although a setback above the original building's fifth floor preserves the proportions of its front elevation.

The buildings acknowledge one another through the complementary proportioning of their fenestration while simultaneously celebrating the contrast between old and new. 114 Hudson's unabashedly contemporary façade consists of curtain wall with intermittent casement windows, and is enhanced by horizontal sunshades at each level. The masonry façade of 116 Hudson has been preserved, with alterations essentially limited to reglazing. The buildings appear most similar at street level, where the old building's three cast-iron bays are filled with the same window wall sported by its new neighbor to the south.

❶ to Franklin St.

4

One York
One York Street (at Sixth Ave.)
Enrique Norten, TEN Arquitectos
2009

The developers of this site inherited an undistinguished Civil-War era brick warehouse. Although they ultimately decided to retain it and preserve its intriguing dialogue with the street grid, they charged the architects with substantially expanding its volume and transforming its appearance. The designers' solution was to insert an elegant, transparent glass tower, which reinterprets the angles established by the existing building and redefines the relationship between its static masonry masses. The setback at the juncture of old and new offers the opportunity (well exploited) for rooftop landscaping.

The addition, which manages to appear grounded and weightless at the same time, contrasts dramatically with the existing building, whose fenestration is rendered as simple punched openings. The mixed-use project contains forty loft units (twenty-five in the original building and the remaining fifteen in the new tower), retail space at street level, and offices on the second floor. The main entrance is on Sixth Avenue.

A C E 1 to Canal St.

5

60 Thompson
60 Thompson Street (at Broome St.)
Stephen B. Jacobs Group, PC
Thomas O'Brien, Aero Studios
2001

This 14-story, 100-room hotel dares to be different, and in surprisingly understated ways. Its conservative brown brick façade is a welcome stylistic departure from conventional "hip" hotel design. The lower two floors are clad in cast stone in a contemporary interpretation of the "rusticated base," while extensive glazing at the two-story penthouse suite serves as the building's crown. The most distinctive architectural feature is the unusual (for New York) series of curved, projecting wrought iron balconies. In response to the narrowness of Thompson Street, the building was set back to afford a view of its elevation from the sidewalk.

The hotel also makes an unusual gift of greenery to the street: in a gracious and unexpected gesture, a pair of small gardens with Eastern overtones flanks the front entrance. The Asian sensibilities continue on the inside, where the David Rockwell-designed Kittichai serves contemporary Thai food. The main lobby, located on the second floor, boasts a visually warm materials palette and a smooth, contemporary vibe.

to Canal St.

6

SoHo Housing
40 Mercer Street (at Grand St.)
Architectures Jean Nouvel
2004

With the supporting star power of architect Jean Nouvel and hotelier Andre Balzacs, this building quickly established itself as the most talked-about new address in SoHo. Thankfully, the architecture measures up: the curtain wall is a robust, vigorous design statement, which benefits from a minimalist color palette and impeccable detailing. (The red and blue glazing is a nod to Piet Mondrian.) The building contrasts with the surrounding nineteenth-century cast iron buildings while at the same time evoking their strength. Its massing is essentially two bold, rectilinear forms, with one dramatic setback at midheight.

In configuring the building, a series of interesting placements was made in order to accommodate the high-fashion (and high-trafficked) location: the residential entry is located on the relatively quiet Mercer Street, while the service entry is placed on the more visible Grand. Bright retail space (which inevitably contrasts with the elegant elevations) fills most of the streetwall at Grand Street and Broadway. The building is set apart from its neighbors by a private outdoor plaza, which faces Broadway and is protected behind story-high glass.

J M Z 6 to Canal St.
N Q R W to Canal St.

7

72 Mercer Street
72 Mercer Street (at Broome St.)
Traboscia Roiatti Architects
2006

This lovely little building manages to be contextual, contemporary, graceful and engaging, all at the same time. This is no small feat in the historic district of SoHo, where all new development is closely scrutinized to ensure that the character of the nineteenth-century neighborhood is preserved. (This project, in fact, was only the second new building in SoHo to be approved by the Landmarks Preservation Commission.) The previous occupant of the narrow 30' x 200' lot, a cast-iron building constructed in the 1860s, had been destroyed by fire some years earlier.

Although the building's two facades are complementary, they are subtly differentiated by their composition and materials. The primary elevation at 501 Broadway features cast stone, while the secondary Mercer Street façade uses brick veneer. Color choices give the elevations a quiet, contemporary feel, without being overly assertive. The building sports modern interpretations of historic details, such as a perforated cornice, and is impeccably proportioned. It contains eight apartments which face a central courtyard.

J M Z 6 to Canal St.
N Q R W to Canal St.

8

Scholastic Building
557 Broadway (at Prince St.)
Aldo Rossi Studio di Architettura
MAP Architect
2000

This project was completed by the office of Italian Rationalist Aldo Rossi after his death. Tucked mid-block in the SoHo historic district, it tips its hat to its nineteenth-century neighbors while retaining its own distinct individuality. The building's two facades showcase a contemporary reinterpretation of such traditional architectural elements as pilasters and cornices: the Broadway elevation presents a formal, colonnaded form, while the rear façade at 130 Mercer is flatter and more industrial in appearance. (See Number 7 for a similar design strategy.)

The use of contrasting colors, architectural lettering, and simple, bold forms evokes a child's set of building blocks, which is especially appropriate given the anchor tenant. The design elements are proportioned so as to maintain the architectural character of the immediate surroundings. The building maintains such harmony with its context that most people fail to notice: it does not contain a single brick!

to Prince St.
6 to Spring St.

9

497 Greenwich Street
497 Greenwich Street (at Spring St.)
Winka Dubbeldam, Archi-Tectonics
2004

This residential building has received much attention for its spectacular folded curtain wall. The regular horizontal pattern of mullions, established at the top and bottom, is foiled by a three-dimensional cascading form which creates, according to the architect, an "inhabitable façade." The curtain wall assertively engages the street and creates a dramatic contrast with the two-dimensional, utilitarian masonry facades typical of the neighborhood. Its complex angles are reinterpreted by secondary elements in the building, such as the balconies and the handrail serving the entrance ramp. Even the canopy over the entrance is part of the curtain wall, and thus becomes part of the building envelope.

The project consists of a renovated existing six-story warehouse as well as the adjacent eleven-story addition; the latter extends over the top of the original building. (See Number 3 for a similar, though far more restrained, design approach.) The meeting of old and new is articulated with crisp, precast balconies, which jut out (like vertical dentils) at regular intervals. The building contains 23 apartments.

to Spring St.
1 to Canal St.

10

505 Greenwich Street
505 Greenwich Street (at Spring St.)
Handel Architects, LLP
2006

This fourteen-story building, which includes 104 residential units, had a tough act to follow, with the attention-grabbing 497 Greenwich Street (Number 9) located immediately to the south. The architects responded by presenting a façade of cool, simple elegance, whose proportions and massing are intended to emulate those of surrounding nineteenth-century industrial buildings. Materials include oxidized copper plate, stainless steel, and precast concrete, which, in the words of the architects, are "refined yet tough."

The imposing through-block building is in an approximate "J" shape. At street level, slotted windows demarcate the lobby, and an expanse of glass showcases the location of the retail tenant. A rhythmic series of copper light boxes is integrated into the second floor level, while at the upper levels, the building's disciplined curtain wall has a complex but regular pattern of mullions. The shorter façade on Renwick Street is similarly treated.

 to Spring St.
1 to Canal St.

11

New Museum
235 Bowery (at Prince St.)
Kazuyo Sejima and Ryue Nishizawa, SANAA
Gensler
2007

This building marked a triumphant return for the museum, which had previously occupied a storefront location on Broadway (in close proximity to the now-defunct Guggenheim SoHo and the now-relocated Museum for African Art). The straightforward architectural concept is that of box-like, windowless galleries stacked in an irregular pattern. This accommodates skylights on each level and gives the building a dynamic profile. The exterior is clad in an oversize version of expanded anodized aluminum mesh. (Unfortunately, Ugo Rondinone's intractably obnoxious "Hell, Yes!" sculpture is apparently intended to become a permanent part of the composition.)

The designers indulged themselves with a sweeping terrace on the top floor, which affords dramatic views of the (for now) much shorter surrounding buildings. Galleries are big, bright and bare, with ceilings of exposed structural steel, and evoke memories of the warehouse galleries once common in the neighborhood. Other program spaces include a gift shop, café, education center, and the 182-seat Peter Jay Sharp Theater.

F V to 2nd Ave.
J M Z to Bowery
6 to Spring St

12

290 Mulberry Street
290 Mulberry Street (at E. Houston St.)
SHoP Architects PC
2009

This thirteen-story residential building contains nine apartments, as well as commercial space on the ground floor. Since zoning requirements dictated that the façade be "predominantly masonry," the architects created a contemporary three-dimensional, articulated brick façade whose proportions draw inspiration from the surrounding nineteenth-century buildings. The rich brown color of the brick lends it a feeling of stability and permanence, while its pattern emphasizes that it is a veneer rather than part of the structure.

Like many of SHoP Architects's designs, this one is based on a dichotomy. The brick façade wraps around the Houston and Mulberry streetwalls, while the south elevation and penthouse provide a contrast both in massing and in cladding.

B D F V to Broadway-Lafayette
6 to Bleecker St.

13

One Kenmare Square
210 Lafayette Street (at Kenmare St.)
Gluckman Mayner Architects
2006

The attention-getting efforts of this project were aided immensely by its prominent placement at the foot of Kenmare Street, where it terminates the corridor feeding into the Williamsburg Bridge. The building's most distinctive feature, of course, is its carefully detailed, undulating eleven-story façade, which displays elegant ribbon windows and dark, heavily textured brick masonry. (The showy configuration is rationalized by the claim that residents' views up Lafayette Street are thus improved.) The street level contrasts dramatically by providing a bright, white showplace for the retail tenant, with the residents' entry discreetly tucked to one side.

The through-block building has a second, narrow façade, only six stories high and considerably more demure, at 51 Crosby Street. Its first floor steps back from the property line to expose four round concrete columns. The upper levels confine themselves to one plane, sport an attractively proportioned grid of punched windows and, like the flamboyant Lafayette Street façade, are clad in brick. The building contains seventy-three apartments.

6 to Spring St.

J M Z to Bowery

14

BLUE Condominium
105 Norfolk Street (at Delancey St.)
Bernard Tschumi Architects
2007

This was one of the most notorious attempts to increase the value of new condominiums in an "up-and-coming" neighborhood by hiring a "starchitect" to create a high-profile building. Put another way, this building wanted attention. It got it. A firestorm of criticism (which missed little but reserved especial disdain for the building's color, bulk and shape) rained down as the building went up. Amusingly, the project already commands less attention than it did initially, simply because other new high-rises continue to go up in the area. However, the arresting color and patterning of the façade remain unique, and are prominently featured in marketing materials for the building.

According to the architect, the controversial form is derived logically from unusual zoning constraints: the project is constructed on a residential lot, but also cantilevers over an existing building on an adjacent commercial lot. As a result of this, two different sets of zoning rules apply to the building, and even the roof profile is defined by the different sky exposure planes for the two sites. The building contains thirty-two apartments.

 to Delancey St.
 to Essex St.

15

Switch Building
109 Norfolk Street (at Delancey St.)
nArchitects, PLLC
2007

This project's location, almost immediately north of the high-profile BLUE Condominium (Number 14), increased the challenge of producing a distinctive, attractive building on a modest scale and budget. The owner emphasized the need to construct the building quickly, and had the additional requirement of providing community space on the ground floor. Zoning regulations dictated that the building's façade be set back five feet from the property line. And all this had to happen in a lot only twenty-five feet wide.

The result is a building whose moniker was inspired by its resemblance to a vertical bank of rocker switches in alternate OFF/ON positions. This effect was achieved quite capably using ordinary materials and construction methods. Each apartment projects 18" from the main façade, gaining back some of the cubic feet lost in the five-foot setback. The seven-story building, which contains five apartments (one a penthouse) and an art gallery on the ground floor, is not only a distinctive addition to the neighborhood, it is undeniably cute.

F to Delancey St.

J M Z to Essex St.

16

Thompson LES
190 Allen Street (at Houston St.)
Rawlings Architects PC
2008

This eighteen-story, 140-room hotel is a strong, masculine addition to the Lower East Side skyline. It benefits from a well-chosen palette of neutrals, effective, dynamic massing, and a rhythmic articulation of balconies and floor levels which contrasts with clean, blank planes. To hear the press tell it, the project struggled across the finish line after seemingly interminable delays; however, the wait was worth it.

Exterior materials consist of curtain wall, metal panels, glass balconies, exposed cast-in-place concrete columns, and elegant granite cladding at street level. The upper portion of the base has full-length glass balconies, which screen a sawtooth façade punctuated by the exposed columns. The balconies are reinterpreted at the upper levels as accentuating elements. The staircase in the tall double-height main lobby leads to a bar, lounge and restaurant (with its own entrance at 187 Orchard Street) on the second floor. The building entrepreneurially includes a separate retail space at 185 Orchard. Other features include a roof garden and a third floor outdoor swimming pool.

F to 2nd Ave.

17

48 Bond Street
48 Bond Street (at Bowery)
Deborah Berke & Partners Architects LLP
GF55 Partners
2008

This elegant 11-story residential building on a busy block of Bond Street features a taut orthogonal facade of flamed charcoal-grey granite, which has an improbable quality of lightness. Large, rhythmic canted bay windows provide visual interest and varying shadow patterns. The facade is proportioned in sympathy with its flanking nineteenth-century neighbors on either side, and like them aligns with the lot line.

The building has two setbacks: one at street level and the other at the roof level of the adjacent buildings. The modest entry vestibule is a small part of a largely featureless glass and zinc curtain wall. The upper portion of the building, above the setback, is articulated quite modestly. The building's fourteen two-bedroom apartments include balconies at the rear.

B D F V to Broadway-Lafayette
6 to Bleecker

18

40 Bond Street
40 Bond Street (at Bowery)
Herzog & de Meuron
Handel Architects, LLP
2008

This is Herzog & de Meuron's first project in New York and their first condominium in the United States. Its aesthetic was designed to grab attention, and succeeded in getting it; the developers were rewarded with a virtual stampede of would-be buyers who helped make the block of Bond between Lafayette and Bowery one of the most talked-about spots in town. The eleven-story building includes 27 loft apartments, a triplex penthouse, and five townhouses with backyards and forecourts.

The building's glass mullions were inspired by the NoHo cast-iron aesthetic common to the neighborhood and are a reinterpretation and softening of that type of rugged, geometric structure. The soda bottle-colored glass was cast in Barcelona, and the spacing of the mullions is subtly varied. The Gaudiesque, 140 foot cast aluminum gate has a graffiti-inspired form, which (according to the architects) was developed by digitally manipulating random scribbles. The gate's motif is repeated throughout the project, most notably in the wavy white Corian which clads the main lobby. The building's massing respects the established streetwall, albeit with one lavishly landscaped setback.

B D F V to Broadway-Lafayette
6 to Bleecker

19

25 Bond Street
25 Bond Street (at Lafayette St.)
BKSK Architects LLP
2008

The architects of this project wished to achieve a sophisticated, contemporary exterior while acknowledging the robust industrial aesthetic common to the nineteenth-century buildings in the surrounding NoHo neighborhood. To that end they created a façade consisting of a double-layered screen wall, which features two types of stone cladding. Visually, the composition has considerable depth and interest: the asymmetrical stone wall plays intriguingly off the regular fenestration of the glass wall behind, and its screening effect manages to be both massive and delicate at the same time. The granite sidewalk facing the building received a sinuous embellishment from sculptor Ken Hiratsuka, who also created a complementary piece for the sumptuous, asymmetrically-placed entry lobby. Also included at street level are a retail space and an entry for below-ground parking.

An unusual aspect of this project is that it was developed by seven owners, who collaborated to construct a condominium of which each would own a part. The result is that the eight-story building contains only nine apartments, of which two were speculatively built.

B D F V to Broadway-Lafayette
6 to Bleecker

20

The Cooper Square Hotel
25 Cooper Square (at E. 6th St.)
Carlos Zapata Studio
Perkins Eastman
2009

With its resemblance to the Burj al-Arab hotel (currently the tallest hotel in the world), this project was quickly dubbed "Dubai on the Bowery." It goes without saying that the neighbors don't like it, presumably because it is tall and clad in fritted white glass. Cooler heads would note that the tower's tapering form is really quite graceful and stylish, and that the impact of its street-level entrance is softened by Nathan Browning's landscaping. The elegant interiors, which utilize sumptuous natural materials to create a quiet, minimalist aesthetic, were designed by Antonio Citterio.

After reversing initial plans to demolish three existing nineteenth-century tenement buildings, the developers incorporated them into the project's design, creating an unusual relationship between old and new. The existing buildings contributed their air rights as well as their first and second floor space. The buildings' two remaining tenants (one a well-known poet), who declined buyout offers, continue to live on the third and fourth floors. The building has 23 floors and 146 rooms (and guests, of course, enjoy dramatic views).

to 8th St.

6 to Astor Pl.

21

Astor Place Towers
445 Lafayette Street (at Astor Place)
Gwathmey Siegel & Associates Architects
2006

With a prominent site at the foot of Astor Place and "starchitect" Charles Gwathmey on board, expectations were high for sales success and a subsequent onslaught of similar projects. For some reason, the end result just didn't quite seem to click with the buying public. As the tallest new building in the neighborhood, it was (predictably) disparaged by the community, but apartment shoppers seemed to turn a cold shoulder as well. The establishment criticized the design for using segmented (rather than curved) glass, and for being too architecturally assertive in the soon-to-be-an-historic-district NoHo neighborhood.

Now that the storm has somewhat abated, a fresh look reveals a strong, dynamic design with skillful massing, balanced use of differentiated wall treatments, and an understated but deft materials palette. (Perplexingly, of the building's four elevations, the one facing north is the least architecturally successful.) In addition, the full-floor apartments, which offer floor-to-ceiling views in three directions, are, by all accounts, quite breathtaking. It would not be at all surprising if the developers were to prove the naysayers wrong in the end.

R W to 8th St.
6 to Astor Pl.

22

173/176 Perry Street
173/176 Perry Street (at Tenth Ave.)

165 Charles Street
165 Charles Street (at Tenth Ave.)
Richard Meier & Partners
2003/2006

The first new building commission in Manhattan for architect Richard Meier, the twin Perry Street towers also benefit from a high-profile location on the West Side. They exhibit the typical Meier "white box" starkness and painstaking attention to elegant detailing. The metal and glass facades are carefully proportioned, and the overall composition is a supremely elegant architectural statement reminiscent of Mies's era-defining 860 Lake Shore Drive towers. Sensibly, the massive cores of the buildings are located on their eastern ends, which opens the western facades to face the Hudson River. Radiant heating is carefully integrated into the curtain wall system.

Three years later, Meier was brought back to design 165 Charles Street, which was conceived as a "blockbuster sequel" to the two earlier buildings. In this case, a central core divides each floor into two two-bedroom apartments, and the lack of balconies gives the tower a more monolithic appearance. Unlike at the earlier buildings, which featured loft-type units, here Meier also designed the apartments' interiors.

23

The Hotel Gansevoort
18 Ninth Avenue (at W. 13th St.)
Stephen B. Jacobs Group, PC
2004

Painfully chic when it opened, this 187-room hotel has (so far) successfully maintained its marketing position in the so-hip-it-hurts Meatpacking District. The north and east sides of the building are wrapped in an enclosed outdoor courtyard, replete with greenery, which serves as outdoor seating for Ono restaurant. (The same architect had similar Asian-inspired leanings at another hotel: see Number 5.) A small retail space with its own street entrance is judiciously tucked in at the northwest corner. The double-height lobby, which epitomizes voguish minimalism, is entered through a 14-foot high revolving door. The building is crowned with a year-round outdoor pool, bar and restaurant, and an event space with 20-foot ceilings.

Like many new buildings, this one is clad in the now-ubiquitous zinc-colored metal panels. It avoids looking conventional thanks in large part to a vigorous composition of projecting bay windows and glass-enclosed Juliet balconies. The building looks even more distinctive at night, when it is enhanced by funky architectural lighting (lots of purple), and the street-level columns are illuminated from within.

 to 14th St.
L to Eighth Ave.

24

The Standard New York
848 Washington Avenue (at W. 13th St.)
Polshek Partnership Architects LLP
2009

A strikingly bold, dynamic architectural statement, this 337-room hotel is a stylistic throwback to the Space Age brutalism of the 1960s, with an exposed concrete structure, narrow profile, and vast areas of curtain wall. The look of the building evokes a "tough but sophisticated" aesthetic based on the work of mid-century modern designers, particularly Morris Lapidus. The concrete pilotis, as well as the irregular patterning of the mullions, inevitably invite comparison to the late work of Le Corbusier.

In a dramatic gesture, the supporting structure straddles the High Line (which the architects apparently either desire or anticipate will remain in place indefinitely). To optimize guests' views, the form of the building is folded, like an open book. Blocky, funky entryways make full use of bold colors as well as of forms inspired by 1970s supergraphics. Playful metal furniture adorns the outdoor plaza, which also serves as a dining area. Other architectural features include a base structure inspired by the historic industrial buildings for which the neighborhood is noted, and a sculptural steel stair. This project succeeded where another failed: a proposed 32-story Jean Nouvel condominium was nixed by the community in 2004.

A C E to 14th St.
L to Eighth Ave.

25

The Porter House
66 Ninth Avenue (at W. 15th St.)
SHoP Architects PC
2003

This project, which contains 22 condominium units, was a renovation of, and addition to, a six-story 1905 warehouse. Characteristically, SHoP Architects decided to emphasize the difference between the old and the new (see also Number 38). Accordingly, the four-story addition is cantilevered eight feet beyond the original building, so that the new building and the addition are each defined as a simple rectilinear mass. (The exception is the addition's southeast corner, which is subtracted to create outdoor space.)

In contrast to the original building's load bearing masonry walls, the addition is clad in zinc panels and includes full height windows. Translucent backlit vertical panels, which dramatically illuminate the façade at night, are interspersed with the windows. (The illumination technique is repeated horizontally in the original building's new wraparound canopy.) The zinc panels also extend downward over one bay of the original building's north façade, like a finger making its mark on what existed before.

A C E to 14th St.
L to Eighth Ave.

26

Chelsea Modern
447 W. 18th Street (at Tenth Ave.)
Audrey Matlock Architects
2006

This dynamic undulating façade, consisting of five horizontal bands of glass, grabbed attention from the moment the architectural rendering was released. Happily, the actual building looks as good or better.

Fixed glazing is blue. Projecting windows are of clear glass and are placed randomly within the façade, creating patterns which change over time as users open and close their windows. The complex form (literally) reflects its surroundings in a way that provides a great deal of visual interest. In contrast with the main façade, the street level façade is rendered as a flat plane of translucent glass with a vertical orientation. The twelve-story building, which contains 47 apartments, sports a relatively modest lobby and eschews a retail tenant in favor of a separate street entry for each ground-floor duplex unit.

A C E to 14th St.
L to Eighth Ave.

27

Four Five Nine
459 W. 18th Street (at Tenth Ave.)
Della Valle Bernheimer
2008

The architects of this building, who also acted as developers for the project, faced the formidable challenge of having as a neighbor the attention-grabbing Chelsea Modern (Number 26). To provide a contrast, the building emphasizes planar geometry, is primarily vertical rather than horizontal, and evinces a strong, confident presence. (For buildings whose designers met similar challenges, see Numbers 10 and 15.)

The anthropomorphic form of the building evokes clasping hands. The duality of its massing is articulated with two contrasting colors of composite aluminum panels, each color with its own distinctive pattern of reveals. Bands of generously-sized ribbon windows temper the verticality of the building and provide expansive views. At street level, an open façade showcases the lobby and a retail tenant, and a wedge-shaped entry canopy evokes the overall form. The eleven-story building contains ten full-floor apartments, each with keyed elevator access.

A C E to 14th St.
L to Eighth Ave.

28

The IAC Building
555 W. 18th Street (at Eleventh Ave.)
Frank Gehry
2007

To date, this is New York City's only building by Frank Gehry, who is probably the best-known living American architect. (Ambitious plans for a Gehry-designed Guggenheim South, which would have been architecturally similar to the Guggenheim Bilbao, were abruptly shelved when the foundation realized it had overextended itself financially.)

A welcome surprise: instead of crumpled titanium, we are presented with a stylish billowing façade of modulating fritted white glass. To some, it evokes the sails of a ship (appropriate to the building's location on the Hudson River); to others, the pleats of a skirt. The building evinces skillful formmaking, which looks dynamic and graceful from all directions. As an added bonus, it is a bold advertisement to drivers on the West Side Highway (see also Number 22). Fortunately for the building's owner, the "IAC" logo complements rather than detracts from the building's architecture.

A C E to 14th St.
L to Eighth Ave.

29

Jim Kempner Fine Art
501 W. 23rd Street (at Tenth Ave.)
Smith and Thompson Architects
1999

This project serves not only as an art gallery but as office space for Smith and Thompson Architects, who designed the project and promptly moved in upon its completion (good for them!). Art is displayed in the basement, first and second floors, as well as in the enclosed courtyard adjacent to the street.

The building presents a complex, Cubist form, which manages to be simultaneously sophisticated and inviting. The major components of its industrial Modernist palette are raw steel, glass, and natural pine. Generous areas of fenestration provide ample daylighting. A walk through the highly varied gallery spaces, which are crammed with constantly-changing art, is always a rewarding experience.

to 23rd St.

30

High Line 519
519 W. 23rd Street (at Tenth Ave.)
Lindy Roy, Roy Co.
2007

This eleven-story residential building is just fun. Faced with a narrow (twenty-five foot) lot adjacent to the High Line, the architect chose a whimsical, stylish treatment for the crucial front and rear elevations. Each floor of the building sports floor-to-ceiling glass, and is visually differentiated with its own door placement and corresponding unique mullion spacing.

The full-floor apartments boast Juliet balconies at the front and full balconies at the rear. Balustrades are freeform perforated stainless steel panels, which further enliven the curtain wall facades. The panels, which sport a subtle honeycomb pattern, evoke the Pop Art supergraphics of the 1970s. A combination of metal and composite panels, in three subtly contrasting colors, clads the east elevation and base of the building.

C E to 23rd St.

31

Chelsea Arts Tower
545 W. 25th Street (at Eleventh Ave.)
Kossar & Garry
Gluckman Mayner Architects
HOK
2007

This building is a "commercial condominium," which means that it consists entirely of office space which was sold rather than leased. Floor plans were sized and proportioned with art galleries in mind, and initial sales were very successful. Two of its art galleries contribute to the vibrant Chelsea street scene: Marlborough Chelsea, whose space includes an outdoor terrace, occupies the first two floors of the main building, while Cheim & Read occupies the single-story adjacent portion at 547 W. 25th. Appropriately for the tenants, the building employs a quiet palette of neutrals, consisting of anodized aluminum curtain wall, composite panels in two colors, and exposed cast-in-place concrete at street level.

At twenty stories and 280 feet, the building is significantly taller than any other in the neighborhood. Shortly after the Department of City Planning approved the project, howls of protest from the neighbors resulted in a hasty rewriting of the zoning ordinance. The new height restriction of 135 feet means that those who own office space in this building will be able to enjoy their views for the foreseeable future.

to 23rd St.

32

37 Arts - Baryshnikov Arts Center
450 W. 37th Street (at Ninth Ave.)
Averitt Associates
Landy Verderame Arianna Architects
TEKArchitects
2005

This theatre complex, unusually, is styled in a contemporary take on Brutalism. Materials consist of exposed structural concrete (bush-hammered at street level), steel and aluminum painted battleship gray, and structural glass infilling the center bay. (The glass reveals the vertical circulation elements, a strategy also utilized by Number 50.) The building's aesthetic is exemplified by its steel entry canopy, supported on two cantilevered concrete beams and enhanced by architectural lettering.

Also unusual is the building's tenant mix, which includes both commercial and non-profit arts organizations. Three commercial theater spaces, owned and operated by a team of producers, occupy the lower floors. The upper three floors, which enjoy spectacular views from the large windows at the rear of the building, are occupied by The Baryshnikov Arts Center. Nonprofit tenant's programs include artist residencies and student fellowships. Sadly, the lead design architect, John W. Averitt, died of cancer at the age of 58 prior to the building's completion.

A C E to 34th St

33

Sky House
11 E. 29th Street (at Fifth Ave.)
FXFowle Architects, PC
2008

This project was initiated by the adjacent Church of the Transfiguration (Episcopal), which purchased the property and utilized its existing air rights to maximize the size of the new building. (Also known as "The Little Church Around the Corner," the church was originally built in 1852 and received additions until 1906.) This presented the architects with a formidable challenge: how to construct, on a very narrow site, a 55-story tower which respected the small-scale church. Impressively, the finished project succeeds with verve and panache.

The entire building is clad in a rich brown brick, whose color was carefully chosen to complement the church. The long, narrow form of the building is broken up into three distinct masses, each of which has a different proportion of masonry to glass. The varying levels of transparency and lightness are further articulated by the use of multiple brick styles. The end result is that the building soars, while at the same time remaining grounded. At street level, a sawtooth, two-story entryway provides a contrasting form and engages the sidewalk. It is all really very handsomely done.

to 23rd St.

34

One Madison Park
22 E. 23rd Street (at Madison Ave.)
Cetra/Ruddy Incorporated
2009

Much maligned for its assertiveness and height, this building, the first new major residential development in the neighborhood, is in truth amazingly elegant, stylish and graceful, given its size and prominent location. The architects made some simple but bold decisions that led to this happy result.

The choice of a basic, orthogonal geometry could easily have led to a visually static, inert tower: not so. A series of rectilinear masses, which project slightly from the main form of the tower, segments the tall shaft into a rhythmic architectonic composition. In addition, the dark facades facing south and west provide a pleasing contrast to the glass walls at the north and east. The proportions of the main tower are sufficiently tall and thin to evoke a sense of wonder, which is rarely conveyed by buildings in the 21st century. With luck, the building will become as beloved as the adjacent Flatiron Building and Met Life Tower, which were also groundbreakingly radical when first constructed.

to 23rd St.
6 to 23rd St.

35

Baruch College
55 Lexington Avenue (at E. 25th St.)
Kohn Pedersen Fox Associates
2005

This building, which contains 40% of Baruch College's total floor area, is frequently described as a "vertical campus." Its shape was driven by zoning regulations, which allowed a medium-rise building, covering the entire site, as an alternative to a tower. Exercising this option maximized the size of each level's floor plate, and eliminated the need for extensive setbacks. The distinctive curved shape of the upper portion of the building is instantly recognizable (and was quickly adapted to create a new logo for the Zicklin School of Business); the form may have been inspired by the nearby Sixty-Ninth Regiment Armory, designed by Hunt & Hunt and completed in 1906. In contrast, the brick and stone base emulates the materials and heights of surrounding buildings.

The program includes a 500-seat lecture hall, theater and athletic facilities, a bookstore, cafeteria, classrooms, and faculty offices. The building is vertically ordered by a series of four-story atria which are stacked diagonally; each school within the building is organized around its own atrium. Technical innovations include a skip-stop elevator system and extensive daylighting.

36

New York City Office of the Chief Medical Examiner (OCME) DNA Forensics Biology Laboratory
520 First Avenue (at E. 26th St.)
Perkins Eastman
2006

Tucked away almost on the East River, this project has received virtually no attention from the architectural tastemakers. However, it is a splendid example of a conventional building catapulted into the realm of the extraordinary by skillful design of ordinary elements.

The architects created a dynamic massing which simultaneously emphasizes verticality and solidity. They enhanced the composition by creating a simple but effective vocabulary which defines each mass: some are solid masonry, some all-glass, and some a combination of the two. Patterns of mullions and ribbons of brick are carefully proportioned. The generous plaza gracing the front manages to be secure and inviting at the same time (are you listening, 7 World Trade Center?). It is hard to point to a single misstep, and the whole composition comes off magnificently. This is especially welcome coming from Perkins Eastman, whom we know for producing handsome, but not always exciting, buildings. This one is a home run.

6 to 28th St.

37

Gramercy 145
145 Lexington Avenue (at E. 29th St.)
Manuel Glas
2009

The action is at the top! The crown of this building is a De Stijl fantasy of interlocking horizontals and verticals, projecting solids and voids, and robust fenestration. Lucky residents, of course, also get to enjoy the roof garden, while the rear façade, sheathed entirely in glass, naturally offers them abundant light and views. In contrast to both the glassy rear elevation and the exuberant crown, less is more when it comes to the front elevation, which presents a quiet grid of regularly spaced punched windows. This simplicity continues at the recessed building entrance, which is defined by polished black granite and protected by a straightforward glass-and-steel canopy (the latter nevertheless suggests the aesthetic of the building's high-spirited upper floors). The building's attractive materials palette also includes warm red brick with carefully matched mortar, black-painted steel, and white-painted exterior soffits.

The project was shoehorned in between two nineteenth-century buildings of four stories each, which, despite dire prognostications, seem to have survived the experience unscathed.

6 to 28th St.

38

M127
127 Madison Avenue (at E. 31st St.)
SHoP Architects PC
2008

This renovation/addition gutted an existing eight-story building and created one loft apartment on each floor. A four-story addition to the top accommodates two duplex penthouses with terraces. As is typical for the work of SHoP Architects, the difference between old and new is accentuated: the addition utilizes zinc panels, similar to those at The Porter House (Number 25), which contrast with the original building's dark masonry walls. The retail space at street level features a large glass window and corresponding glass door. The white tenant door includes glazing with vertical supergraphics spelling out the name of the project.

The building's most interesting feature is its angled windows inserted into the existing masonry openings. These create seating nooks, provide views down Madison Avenue, and create visual interest. (The angled windows are expressed similarly in both the addition and the original building, but face in different directions!)

6 to 28th St.

39

The Morgan Library & Museum Addition
225 Madison Avenue (at E. 37th St.)
Renzo Piano Building Workshop
Beyer Blinder Belle Architects & Planners
2006

This is the second—and more successful—attempt to unify the disparate buildings of the Morgan Library campus with a new enclosed glass court (the first effort, by Voorsanger & Mills, proved too modest and stood for less than ten years). Granting that it obviously benefited from a generous budget, Renzo Piano's design succeeds brilliantly at consolidating the campus and at providing a variety of much-needed new spaces, as well as an attractive main entrance. Although zoning regulations would have allowed a relatively tall addition, it was deliberately kept low in deference to the existing buildings. (Additional cubic footage was gained by excavating to create a full story below grade.) At the interior, warm wood contrasts with the crisp steel and glass, and architectural detailing throughout is absolutely flawless.

The existing complex consisted of three buildings. J.P. Morgan's private library (designed in 1906 by Charles McKim of McKim Mead and White) was expanded in 1928 by the Benjamin W. Morris addition to the west. The third building, completed in 1853, was at one time owned by a member of Morgan's family and was subsequently purchased by the museum.

6 to 33rd St.

40

Scandinavia House
58 Park Avenue (at E. 37th St.)
Polshek Partnership Architects LLP
2000

In an interview, James Stewart Polshek described the opportunity to design a building which would make a strong architectural statement while showcasing the long history of the Scandinavian design tradition. The site, barely fifty feet wide, previously contained two townhouses. The initial plan was to tear down one and renovate the other; an addition would concurrently be constructed on the site of the demolished building. It was ultimately decided that a completely new building was the best aesthetic and functional solution.

The façade is clad in zinc panels, spruce, and glass, with an emphasis on deep reveals, horizontality, and careful detailing. The "Scandinavia House" lettering provides a contrasting vertical element, and decorative flags are used effectively at the base. Inside, furnishings are by Scandinavian designers such as Arne Jacobsen, Bruno Mathsson and Alvar Aalto. The ground floor, open to the public, includes a café and gift shop.

6 to 33rd St.

41

425 Fifth Avenue
425 Fifth Avenue (at E. 38th St.)
Michael Graves & Associates
H. Thomas O'Hara Architect, PLLC
2003

Although Michael Graves is a master at designing whimsical architectural details (as well as teakettles), his buildings sometimes suffer from a repetitive heaviness which gives them a static quality. This one is a welcome exception.

The base, although it exhibits a bit of the characteristic Gravesian clunkiness, can nevertheless boast of a friendly engagement with the street. The tower, however, which erupts joyously toward the heavens, is indisputably masterful. The materials palette (which includes limestone, metal panels, and brick cladding), subtle setbacks, and a careful balancing of horizontal and vertical elements all contribute to a confidently warm and exuberant composition. New York has few PoMo buildings (construction in the city was in a bit of a lull when the style was in vogue) but this one is, without a doubt, the best.

B D F V to 42nd St.-Bryant Park
7 to 5th Ave.

42

New York Public Library
Humanities and Social Sciences Library
South Court
476 Fifth Avenue (at W. 42nd St.)
Davis Brody Bond
2005

Completed in 1911, the main branch of the New York Public Library was designed by Carrere & Hastings and is generally considered the high point of Beaux-Arts design in New York City. Extensive renovations to the building began in 1985. This project, along with the restoration of the main reading room on the third floor, is the most welcome result to date.

The architects wished to create a modern addition which would not compromise the integrity of the original building. To that end, the bijou-like infill structure, which occupies a former enclosed courtyard, was pulled back from the existing and a skylight was provided around the entire perimeter. This not only left the former exterior walls exposed to view, but created the opportunity to daylight the entire new interior. A glass staircase, which leads down one level to the auditorium, reveals the original foundation walls (in order to limit the height of the building to three stories, additional space was created by excavating.) The program also includes a teaching center, offices, and an employee lounge.

B D F V to 42nd St.-Bryant Park
7 to 5th Ave.

43

505 Fifth Avenue
505 Fifth Avenue (at E. 42nd St.)
Kohn Pedersen Fox Associates
2006

This is one of a dozen or so major projects which was put on hold immediately following 9/11. Existing buildings on the site (one of which, astoundingly, was only one story), sat condemned and vacated for approximately two years before the developers finally made the decision to move forward. But the wait was worth it. The building is a fitting anchor to the most famous crossroads in the world, and keeps good company with the soaring 500 Fifth and the sumptuous New York Public Library. (At some point, with luck, the undistinguished building at the southeast corner will be replaced with a more praiseworthy occupant.)

Tenants, of course, enjoy expansive views of some of the most famous buildings in the city. Recognizing this, the architects pulled the perimeter columns back from the façade to allow the curtain wall to continue uninterrupted around the perimeter. The building itself has a pleasing, angular form, and capably accommodates the inevitable retail space at its base. At only 27 stories, it is, by Midtown standards, quite modest in size.

B D F V to 42nd St.-Bryant Park
7 to 5th Ave.

44

Bank of America Tower
One Bryant Park (W. 42nd St. at Sixth Ave.)
Cook + Fox Architects
Gensler
2009

On December 15, 2007, the 54-story, 1,200 foot Bank of America Tower became the second-tallest in New York when its 255-foot spire was put in place. As its name indicates, the building is the headquarters for the Bank of America, which occupies the majority of the floor space. (Its site had previously been assembled by the Durst family over a forty-year period.) In defiance of the shaky marketplace, the building was, according to its developers, 98% leased eight months before scheduled completion.

The building's faceted form, evocative of a crystal structure, was designed to meet zoning and organizational requirements as well as to open desirable views. The north façade incorporates the façade of the demolished 1918/1928 Henry Miller's Theatre, whose programmatic components were reconstructed in the new building. A one-acre green roof opens space between the tower and the adjacent Condé Nast building (Number 53). Much-publicized "sustainable" features include coated glass to reduce heat gain, a co-generation and ice storage system, an advanced graywater/stormwater management system, and materials which have been carefully selected for recycled content.

B D F V to 42nd St.-Bryant Park
7 to 5th Ave.

45

Harvard Club of New York City
27 W. 44th Street (at Fifth Ave.)
Davis Brody Bond
2004

The original Harvard Club, designed by McKim, Mead & White in 1894, was one of the first buildings to be designated a New York City landmark (in 1967), and had been previously expanded in 1905, 1915 and 1947. Faced with dark red brick and limestone trim in a "colonial revival" style which evokes the Cambridge campus, the venerable building is one of the most revered members of the famed "club row" between Fifth and Sixth Avenues. This meant that the prospect of an eight story addition invited intense scrutiny from preservationists.

The magnificent new building is clad in limestone and bronze-colored curtain wall, the latter framed on three sides with the fourth side left open to acknowledge the original building to the east. The building also successfully engages the equally significant New York Yacht Club to its west, which was designed by Warren and Wetmore in 1900. The program includes dining and meeting rooms, guest bedrooms, athletic facilities, administrative offices, a library, a bar, and lounges.

B D F V to 42nd St.-Bryant Park
7 to 5th Ave.

46

Austrian Cultural Forum
11 E. 52nd Street (at Fifth Ave.)
Raimund Abraham
2002

This small (by Midtown standards) building nevertheless commands attention, thanks in no small part to its unusual proportions: 280 feet of height and twenty-four stories in only a twenty-five foot width. The design is the result of a competition, which attracted 226 entries, held by the Republic of Austria. Raimund Abraham's winning entry, selected in 1992, was finally completed ten years later. Among other monikers (guillotine, thermometer, metronome, dagger blade), the building has been likened to a "totem pole," which seems an apt metaphor for such a vertical, segmented, anthropomorphic structure.

The building exhibits strong forms and a spare materials palette. Its three vertical elements have been described by the architect as "the mask," "the core" and "the vertebra." The mask is, of course, the glass façade. The vertebra is the scissor fire stair at the rear, whose placement allows the program spaces (the core) to occupy the entire width of the site. The director's apartment, which occupies the 16th through the 19th floors, projects assertively from the shaft of the building.

47

American Folk Art Museum
45 W. 53rd Street (at Sixth Ave.)
Tod Williams Billie Tsien + Associates
2001

The attention-getting feature of this building is its sixty-three façade panels, which are made of Tombasil (a proprietary white bronze with 57% copper content). These panels, which are folded inward to make the façade appear inviting, were cast using steel and concrete surfaces as formwork. The Tombasil material has the characteristics of fissuring unpredictably as it cools (which individualizes each panel despite the use of identical molds) and of exhibiting a warm glow under morning and evening lighting conditions. The panels generated sufficient advance excitement that one was exhibited, during the building's construction, at the next-door Museum of Modern Art.

Although the building is quite modest in size (eighty-five feet, eight stories) it has a remarkably solid, imposing presence. Its elegant, coolly detached architecture is curiously incongruous with the rustic art which is typically displayed in the galleries. (This leads to the inevitable questioning of the appropriateness of placing a folk art museum in midtown Manhattan. For a more authentic folk art experience, visit the Museum of Appalachia in Norris, Tennessee.) The entire interior is daylit.

  to 5th Ave./53rd St.

48

Apple Store Fifth Avenue
767 Fifth Avenue (at E. 59th St.)
Bohlin Cywinski Jackson
Moed de Armas & Shannon, Architects
2006

This project is a happy ending to a long saga which began with the construction of Edward Durell Stone's iconic GM building in 1968. At that time, the zeitgeist dictated a street wall setback and an expansive plaza, which in this case was sunk below street level. The arrangement was witheringly criticized for destroying the proportions of Grand Army Plaza across Fifth Avenue, and in fact the plaza was never happily integrated into its urban context. The subsequent 1998 sale of the building to a consortium of investors (including Donald Trump) resulted in the total reconstruction of the plaza and its conversion to retail space; which, unfortunately, was never leased.

The current iteration was born of the building's changing hands yet again in 2004 (at a price of $1.4B, then the highest ever for an office building). It is an elegant glass bijou which is a triumph of style, simplicity and sophistication, consisting of a 32-foot glass cube identified by the unmistakable Apple logo. One level below the plaza, the store, open 24/7, is reached by a stunning glass spiral staircase which winds around a cylindrical elevator.

N R W to 5th Ave./59th St.

49

LVMH Tower
19-21 E. 57th Street (at Madison Ave.)
Christian de Portzamparc
The Hillier Group
1999

Was the Louis Vuitton-Moët Hennessy Tower the one that started it all? Maybe, and it certainly was an appropriate statement for a company which produces such luxury unnecessaries as cosmetics, perfumes, luggage, and champagne. Christian de Portzamparc's folded glass design caused a sensation when unveiled, and has since inspired a generation of Revit-armed designers to carve rectilinear forms into crystalline fantasies (see Number 44 for the most high-profile example to date). With typically French logic, the shapes were justified as a rational response to New York City zoning requirements (see also Number 14).

Ironically, the building's design was, by all accounts, arrived at by that most traditional of design tools: the cardboard study model. (Eight or so of the early models were exhibited at the Municipal Art Society's Urban Center while LVMH was under construction.) Despite its relatively modest size (23 stories in a sixty-foot width) the shape, which is frequently compared to that of a lily, gives the impression of a much larger, taller building and conveys a commanding street presence.

N R W to 5th Ave./59th St.

50

59E59 Theatres
59 E. 59th Street (at Madison Ave.)
Leo Modrcin, uRED Architecture
Franke, Gottsegen, Cox Architects
2004

This adaptive reuse project is a terrific example of a building as advertisement. It succeeds largely by celebrating its vertical circulation elements, and thereby showcasing its users every evening. Industrial steel, semi-transparent main stairs are sandwiched between the building's curtain wall façade and its performance spaces. As a result, theatergoers are on display as they move up and down, and as they pause at the small but stylish bar at midlevel.

The façade, which is lit at night and festooned with colorful posters, has an exaggerated verticality which helps the building to assert itself amid taller neighbors. The building's entryway, which integrates its chic "59E59" logo, is tucked under the first stair run. The three theaters (simply lettered off as A, B and C) are of different sizes and configurations to accommodate a variety of productions.

to 5th Ave./59th St.

51

The Bloomberg Tower
One Beacon Court
731 Lexington Avenue (at E. 58th St.)
Cesar Pelli & Associates
2005

After closing its stores, the now-defunct Alexander's department store chain realized that its biggest asset was real estate, and that the crown jewel was the block bounded by Lexington, Third, 58th and 59th Streets. Accordingly, they partnered with a developer to maximize the return on their holdings. After multiple delays and false starts, the triumphant end result is a stunning 54-story, 806-foot building, which is a commanding new presence on the midtown skyline.

Bloomberg LLP occupies the commercial floors, while floors above 31 consist of luxury apartments. Multiple retail stores and a new subway station entrance have been happily incorporated around the perimeter of the building. Separate entries for the offices, residences, and the latest incarnation of Le Cirque (which was previously located at the Villard Houses) are provided within a sumptuous motorcourt, known as Beacon Court, located midblock.

4 5 6 to 59th St.
N R W to Lexington Ave/59th St.

52

The Reuters Building
Three Times Square (Seventh Ave. btwn W. 42nd/43rd Sts.)
Fox & Fowle Architects PC
2001

This 32-story building was constructed as the New York headquarters for Reuters, and is conceptually very similar to the Condé Nast Building (Number 53) designed by the same architects one year earlier. At its southwest, the building is tasked with turning the world-famous corner of Seventh Avenue and West 42nd Street. It accomplishes this with a curved curtain wall which interrupts the main granite-clad, rectilinear form. At the top, this curtain wall is intersected by a fin, which includes curiously subtle signage announcing the name of the building.

At street level, the same corner is faced with terra-cotta cladding (replete with pilasters!) which recalls the ornate treatments of the older Times Square theatres. The base along 42nd Street, of course, includes retail space and elaborate digital signage, as well as a festive subway entrance. At 43rd Street, the building presents a sedate, businesslike face, which includes an entrance for the New Victory Theatre next door. The tenant entrance is on Seventh Avenue.

N Q R W S to Times Square-42nd St.
1 2 3 7 to Times Square-42nd St.

53

Condé Nast Building
Four Times Square (W. 42nd St. at Broadway)
Fox & Fowle Architects PC
2000

This 48-story building is the first of a remarkable quartet of high-rises (see also Numbers 52, 54 and 55) which opened with amazing rapidity in four successive years. Of the four buildings, it is the only one which does not include a subway entrance. It does, however, include a dazzling media wall above the entrance to NASDAQ, which it houses. (The punched windows, which ensure a pattern of holes in every digital advertisement, were reportedly added after prospective tenants complained about the lack of views.)

Like The Reuters Building, Condé Nast was conceived as a duality to reflect both its corporate function and its relationship to Times Square. The facades at the eastern end of the building are therefore clad in granite with regular punched windows, while the western facade features a dramatic curved curtain wall. The spectacular through-block tenant lobby features a pillowy, cascading silver ceiling (clearly visible from the street) and complementary entrances with freestanding canopies on 42nd and 43rd Streets. The building's crown features large panels proclaiming its address. The base is, naturally, crammed with exuberant commercial tenants and plastered with digital signage.

N Q R W S to Times Square-42nd St.
1 2 3 7 to Times Square-42nd St.

54

Ernst & Young
Five Times Square (Seventh Ave. btwn W. 41st/42nd Sts.)
Kohn Pedersen Fox Associates
2002

This 38-story building, which fills an entire block, is clad in visually heavy horizontal bands of glass and metal panels. Happily, the building's regularity is broken up by angularities both in its massing and in the handling of its surface features. The front and rear facades are both broken into angled planes, although the treatment is perhaps a bit too subtle. The diagonal illuminated shaft on the front façade, and the enormous truss mounted to the east elevation (which sports illuminated "Ernst & Young" signage), are more visually successful. Neon signage at the top proclaiming "EY" is also effective.

In addition to the jubilant subway entrance, the base has the usual complement of retail tenants and bright digital signage which is de rigueur for a Times Square building. (Illuminated signage, in fact, has been officially recognized as an essential part of the theatre district's streetscape. The city zoning ordinance now requires inclusion of such signage on any new building project fronting Seventh Avenue or Broadway between 43rd and 50th Streets.) The modest tenant entry is located on Seventh Avenue.

N Q R W S to Times Square-42nd St.
1 2 3 7 to Times Square-42nd St.

55

The Times Square Tower
Seven Times Square (Broadway btwn W. 41st/42nd Sts.)
Skidmore, Owings and Merrill LLP
2003

This was the last of the four new Times Square high-rises to be constructed (see also Numbers 52, 53 and 54), is the most conservatively designed, and is the only one which is freestanding. The elevations of the trapezoidal shape, which rises uninterruptedly for 47 stories, are treated with two juxtaposed curtain wall patterns (one horizontal and one diagonal). Neither treatment is sufficiently large in scale to adequately break up, or add interest to, such vast facades. The building is redeemed by its front elevation, in which the curtain wall—yes!—is recessed to expose the trussed steel structure. At the building's base are retail tenants and a spacious, inviting subway entrance. The tenant entrance, located on Broadway, features a tall clear-glassed lobby and a wedge-shaped entry canopy which visually reaches toward 42nd Street.

This building is the only one of the four towers which was completed and opened without benefit of a namesake anchor tenant: Arthur Andersen, who signed as primary lessor in October 2000, was forced to back out in 2002 after the Enron scandal essentially destroyed the company. The truss mounted to the east elevation looks a bit forlorn as it waits for a namesake tenant to bestow signage.

N Q R W S to Times Square-42nd St.
1 2 3 7 to Times Square-42nd St.

56

The New 42nd Street Studios
229 W. 42nd Street (btwn Seventh/
Eighth Aves.)
Platt Byard Dovell White Architects LLP
2000

This ten-story building, which serves non-profit theater and dance groups, houses fourteen rehearsal studios and a 199-seat black box theatre ("The Duke"). At street level, three separate entryways are provided to serve the performance/ rehearsal spaces, a food retailer, and the renamed American Airlines Theatre next door.

The building's most impressive feature is its architectural lighting, which was developed in collaboration with theatre lighting designer Anne Militello of Vortexlighting. In meeting the neighborhood zoning requirements for an illuminated façade, the designers made an early decision to eschew conventional Times Square advertising lights in favor of making the entire building a glowing, multicolored display. The result is a breathtaking array of slowly morphing lights which bathes the building in a modulating, constantly changing glow, and hints at the performances taking place within. The 175-foot vertical "light wand" at the west of the building was designed in collaboration with James Carpenter (see also Numbers 61 and 89). An extensive catwalk system, slipped behind an elaborate architectural screen, provides access for maintenance.

A C E to 42nd St.-Port Authority
Bus Terminal

57

The New York Times Building
620 Eighth Avenue (at W. 40th St.)
Renzo Piano Building Workshop
FXFowle Architects PC
2006

Announced on December 13, 2001, this project reiterated The New York Times Co.'s commitment to its namesake square and established the prospect of a spectacular New York high-rise designed by Renzo Piano. In the wake of Kelo v. New London, the project was quickly controversial due to the (public) Empire State Development Corporation's role of assembling the site and subsequently leasing it to the developers for 99 years. (In an unfortunate coda to the project, the beleaguered company recently took out a mortgage against the building in order to cover its own operating losses.)

At 1,046 feet, the building is currently tied with the Chrysler Building for the third tallest in New York. The most distinctive feature of its impeccably detailed facade is a series of horizontal 1 5/8" ceramic rods which serve as sunshades. The rods' spacing increases from the base to the top, which gives the upper portion of the structure greater visual transparency. The feature proved useful in facilitating the actions of three climbers who scaled the building in the summer of 2008. The owners are currently experimenting with various means to thwart thrillseekers who intend to use the building as a ladder.

A C E to 42nd St.-Port Authority Bus Terminal

58

The Westin
270 W. 43rd Street (at Eighth Ave.)
Arquitectonica Architects
2002

This 45-story, 863-room hotel probably divides opinion as sharply as does any building in the city. To some, it is the epitome of soaring New York exuberance; to others, it is perversely ugly and crassly commercial. What is certain is that it is designed to grab attention. The building's base is clad in earth-toned metal panels which include regular punched windows. The tower is clad in a multicolored glass curtain wall, and is divided into two parts (one with a horizontal emphasis, one with a vertical) which are articulated by a dramatic illuminated arc.

The designers bowed to the demands of Times Square pedestrian traffic by giving over the W. 42nd Street and Eighth Avenue frontage to entrances for the incredible quantity of retail stores, restaurants and movie theaters (!) housed by the building. Although the hotel can also be accessed from W. 42nd Street, its surprisingly understated main entrance is located one block north. The street-level W. 43rd Street lobby is a daylit four-story sliver of space, while the subdued, urbane main lobby is located on the second floor.

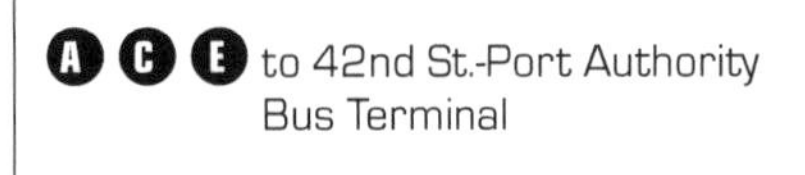

59

785 Eighth Avenue
785 Eighth Avenue (at W. 48th St.)
Ismael Leyva Architects
2009

Rising above the "messy vitality" that is Eighth Avenue west of Times Square, this gorgeously detached building is distinguished by dramatic proportioning and bold contrasts. Improbably tall and thin, its geometry takes advantage of the wedge-shaped site to create a dynamic, asymmetrical form. The disciplined glass curtain wall on the south elevation contrasts with the angular unfenestrated wall which faces north.

The project contains 110 condominium units in forty floors. All units above the eighth floor have elegant blue-glassed balconies, which are angled across the face of the east façade, and on the west façade zoom straight up. Sensibly, the entrance to the ground floor retail space is on Eighth Avenue, while the residential lobby is accessed from 48th Street.

to 50th St.

60

Hearst Tower
300 W. 57th Street (at Eighth Ave.)
Foster + Partners
2006

At long last, this breathtaking structure fulfills Buckminster Fuller's vision for architectural design (and is a triumphant finale to a long series of unbuilt projects by multiple architects, most notably Louis I. Khan's Philadelphia City Hall). The building is also the realization of a never-built skyscraper: the original Hearst Magazine Building, Joseph Urban's six-story Vienna Secessionist Art Deco structure, never received its planned crowning tower after its 1928 completion.

The new 42-story tower is set back from the old streetwall. It is surrounded by a skirt of glass which skylights the interior of the original building and gives the tower the appearance of floating above its base. (Peer in at the daylit main lobby and its glass waterfall feature, bisected by escalators.) The bold decision to create a triangulated, rather than a rectilinear, structure resulted in not only a spectacular form but in a 20% reduction in needed structural steel. The impeccably detailed curtain wall unabashedly expresses the dramatic structure. Unfortunately, the backlash against the Landmarks Preservation Commission for allowing this project to go forward has resulted in a new level of conservatism for the agency.

A B C D to 59th St.-Columbus Circle
1 to 59th St.-Columbus Circle

61

Time Warner Center
10 Columbus Circle
Skidmore, Owings and Merrill LLP
2004

Originally called AOL Time Warner Center, the building's name was quietly changed in 2003, along with that of the company, as AOL's fortunes faded. The project was conceived as a spectacular corporate headquarters, and takes full advantage of its prominent site on Columbus Circle. The building, which embraces the plaza with (almost literally) open arms, is much more happily integrated with its surroundings now that the reconstruction of Columbus Circle (designed by the Olin Partnership) has, finally, been completed.

The building's base includes extensive public retail and restaurant facilities on multiple floors, as well as performance space for Jazz @ Lincoln Center. The base also incorporates new subway station entrances as well as underground parking, and the magnificent main atrium features an astoundingly transparent curtain wall designed by James Carpenter. The upper portion of the building is in the traditional "twin-towered" configuration of Central Park West apartment buildings and includes, in addition to Time Warner's corporate offices, television studios (for CNN), the Mandarin Oriental Hotel, and residential condominiums.

A B C D to 59th St.-Columbus Circle
1 to 59th St.-Columbus Circle

62

Clinton Cove Park Pier 96 Boathouse
Pier 96 (Twelfth Ave. at W. 56th St.)
Dattner Architects
2006

This public facility, owned by the New York City Department of Parks and Recreation, offers kayak rentals for daytrips on the Hudson River. Inspired by the building's nautical pedigree, the simple materials palette consists of wood, stainless steel, corrugated metal panels, and galvanized structural steel. The gently sloping roof (which although conventionally constructed evokes the form of a hyperbolic paraboloid) raises itself slightly above the rectilinear form of the building in order to provide clerestory daylighting. Extensive use of rolling doors allows the building to be opened to the outside during the summer season.

The lawn to the east of the building features Malcolm Cochran's "Private Passage," a 29-foot wine bottle clad in bronze and zinc with a dark green patina. Inside is a stainless steel reproduction of a cabin from the original Queen Mary, which at one time docked at this location. The sculpture's daylit interior, which is intended to evoke the quality of a period photograph, is electrically illuminated at night.

A B C D to 59th St.-Columbus Circle
1 to 59th St.-Columbus Circle

63

Rose Center for Earth and Space
Central Park West and W. 79th Street
Polshek Partnership Architects LLP
2000

The Frederick Phineas and Sandra Priest Rose Center for Earth and Space is noteworthy for the speed with which it was realized: according to the museum, the total time from conception to completion did not exceed five years. Its highly visible centerpiece is the 87-foot diameter Hayden Sphere, occupied by the new Hayden Planetarium and the audio-visual presentation The Big Bang. Exhibits surrounding the sphere were designed by Ralph Appelbaum Associates, and include the Scales of the Universe walkway, the Harriet and Robert Heilbrunn Cosmic Pathway, the Cullman Hall of the Universe and the Gottesman Hall of Planet Earth. The project also includes a new visitor entrance as well as underground parking.

The transparent cube generated tremendous excitement even before it was completed. Upon opening, it instantly became one of the most popular interior spaces in the city. The museum has taken full advantage by regularly hosting parties and private events in the space, which has also been prominently featured in movies such as *Spider-Man 2*. Boullée would be proud.

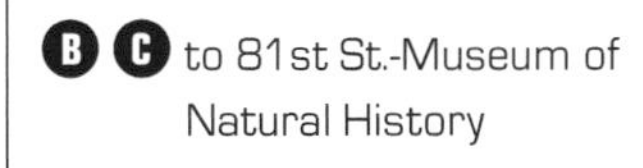

64

Ariel East
2628 Broadway (at W. 99th St.)
Cetra/Ruddy Incorporated
2008

This building is one of a pair of residential towers which were commissioned simultaneously and now face each other across Broadway. According to the towers' developer, they were named after a star (although a quick check reveals that there is as yet no star called Ariel. The celestial body with this moniker is a moon of Uranus, which was named after the sylph in Alexander Pope's The Rape of the Lock). The towers are by different architects but share some aesthetic similarities. Both make use of terra cotta (in three colors) with a distinctive horizontal pattern, as well as granite cladding at street level. Ariel East contains sixty-four condominiums in thirty-seven stories, and has the form of a terraced tower, mostly in glass, but with terra cotta accents.

The Upper West Side between 96th Street and Columbia University, which had seen significant development after 1904 (when the subway was completed) and again in the 1920s, had remained relatively dormant since then. These buildings were the first major projects to be constructed in the neighborhood in many years, and their size and height touched off a firestorm of protests.

to 96th St.

65

Ariel West
245 W. 99th Street (at Broadway)
Cook + Fox Architects
2008

The larger of a pair of towers (see Number 64), Ariel West contains seventy-three condominiums in thirty-one stories. It has a relatively simple form of two rectilinear masses, one set behind the other, and a regular patterning of fenestration in a mostly glass façade. The building sports three colors of terra cotta, with varying color combinations to visually differentiate portions of the building. The street level facing Broadway is given over to retail tenants, while the residential entrance is discreetly tucked around the corner on West 99th Street.

The developer's purchase of air rights from neighboring properties enabled the towers to rise to their imposing height. Complaints against the project resulted in the local community board's voting to rezone a total of fifty-one blocks between 96th and 110th Streets. The change limits the height of buildings on Broadway to 145 feet and prohibits the transfer of air rights from side streets. Like the occupants of the Chelsea Arts Tower (Number 31), therefore, residents of the new buildings should be able to enjoy their views uninterrupted for some time to come.

66

Alfred Lerner Hall
2620 Broadway (at W. 114th St.)
Bernard Tschumi Architects
Gruzen Samton
1999

The starting point for the architecture of this building was Columbia University's master plan for its nineteenth-century campus, which dictated that masonry cladding be used for the east and west wings. Accordingly, these portions of the building were conservatively designed, down to the Flemish bond brick pattern, which mimics that of the campus's McKim, Mead and White buildings. (In addition to brick, the materials palette includes cast stone and pink granite.) In dramatic contrast with the two sedate flanking wings is the connecting six-story atrium, which contains an elaborate system of staggered ramps. Suspended on a carefully designed truss structure, the ramps animate the space with the movement which occurs along them. A curtain wall brings light into the space and engages the adjacent university quad.

As Tschumi stated, the building is "quiet on the outside, and dynamic on the inside." It intriguingly juxtaposes old and new, solid and void, heavy and light. The program includes an auditorium, meeting rooms, dining halls, a bookstore, clubs, and student lounges.

❶ to 116th St.

67

Harlem Children's Zone (HCZ) and Promise Academy
35 E. 125th Street (at Madison Ave.)
Davis Brody Bond
2005

In the last fifteen years there has been an explosion of new projects along 125th Street, proclaiming the area's dramatic resurgence as a desirable commercial location. The majority of the new buildings, while handsome, lack architectural distinction. This project, for a non-profit community facility, is a welcome exception.

The building houses the Promise Academy Charter School, a medical clinic, a community center, and administrative offices. It features a transparent first floor, which engages the community with the activities going on inside the center. A well-chosen palette of materials, including metal panels and three colors of brick, projects the right balance of warmth and exuberance. Fenestration is carefully proportioned, and the massing achieves a dynamic interplay of solid and void.

2 3 to 125th St.
4 5 6 to 125th St.

68

Memorial Sloan-Kettering Mortimer B. Zuckerman Research Center

415 E. 68th Street (at First Ave.)
Skidmore, Owings and Merrill LLP
Zimmer Gunsul Frasca Partnership
2008

This project began development in the mid-1990s, when the adjacent St. Catherine of Siena Church sold its air rights to the Memorial Sloan-Kettering Hospital. The resulting 420-foot, 23-story building is the first of a two-phase expansion. The center's focus on cancer treatment integrates cancer research with patient care, fostering dialogue between scientists, laboratory researchers, and patient care physicians. The building's proximity to the hospital allows an exchange of ideas and a sharing of facilities.

Visually, the project benefits from skilled massing and a striking architectural vocabulary, which includes fritted glass in a checkerboard pattern, elegant sun control devices, and ruddy terra cotta at the base which grounds the building by emphasizing horizontality. The attractive main lobby, with a sculptural stainless steel ceiling, is at 410 E. 69th Street. The building also incorporates a new rectory serving St. Catherine, with its own entry at 411 E. 68th Street. Designed by Acheson Doyle Partners, the rectory includes offices, a parish hall, and a priory for nine priests.

6 to 68th St.

69

Weill Greenberg Center
1305 York Avenue (at E. 70th St.)
Polshek Partnership Architects LLP
2007

This imposing, monolithic building is uniformly clad in white ceramic fritted glass curtain wall and rises straight up without setbacks. Its visual impact is softened by the gentle folding of its façade into diagonal facets, which gives the building a crystalline quality. According to the architect, the façade was conceived as a "diaphanous skin" and was intended as a nod to the 20th century Gothic motifs present in the original New York Hospital campus across the street. The folding pattern is emulated by the wraparound entry canopy and even by the granite pavers at the stepped entrance. In a surprising contrast, the main lobby is quiet and orthogonal, with blonde wood on the walls and travertine on the floor.

Departments housed include dermatology, hypertension, ear nose and throat, in-vitro fertilization, and cardiology. The building also includes a Clinical Skills and Teaching Center. The project is the first phase in what is intended to be an entirely new campus for the Weill Cornell Medical College.

6 to 68th St.

70

The Reece School
25 E. 104th Street (at Fifth Ave.)
Platt Byard Dovell White Architects LLP
2008

This non-profit special education elementary school was founded by Ellen S. Reece in 1948 and currently serves approximately 100 students, aged five to thirteen, who have a variety of learning disabilities. The new building heralds the growth of the school's programs, which were originally housed in neighborhood brownstones. In order to create a facility that would respond to the unique needs of the students, the architects worked closely with teachers, therapists and social workers.

The building contains five stories plus a full basement, and color-coding is used throughout its interior. Program elements include a half-court gymnasium, a rear play terrace, special-use classrooms, quiet rooms, therapy rooms, offices, and non-programmed space. The building's most prominent exterior feature is its playful multicolored glass curtain wall, which differentiates classrooms from each other (and over the course of the day) by bringing in variegated natural light. The glass façade projects slightly but definitively from the quiet masonry streetwall, and assists in scaling the building to its residential surroundings.

6 to 103rd St.

71

York Street Office Addition
110 York Street (at Jay St.)
Scarano Architects PLLC
2005

There has been quite a bit of construction in the recently-christened DUMBO (Down Under the Manhattan Bridge Overpass) neighborhood in the past few years, but this project, one of the earliest, is the most fun. When considering how to add on to this 19th century warehouse, the designers were struck by the contrast between the prosaic, load-bearing masonry building and the exuberant, 1909 steel bridge structure, amazingly only twenty feet away. They therefore decided to, while retaining as much of the existing building as possible, create an addition which would embrace the adjacent bridge and increase the tension between the existing and the new.

The addition is designed to serve as a learning laboratory for architectural design. It features a wide variety of materials, over one hundred types of structural steel connections, and multiple types of curtain wall. Its most striking feature is the dramatically angled, exposed steel truss roof structure, which creates a dialogue with the massive bridge structure (and which can be closely examined from the bridge's bicycle path).

to York St.

72

14 Townhouses
267, 267A, 269, 269A, 271, 273, 275, 277, 279, 281, 283, 285, 285A, and 287 State Street (at Smith St.)
Rogers Marvel Architects, PLLC
DeLaCour & Ferrarra Architects
2007

These fourteen townhouses along the north side of State Street, near downtown Brooklyn, epitomize understated, elegant refinement. It would be hard to imagine a project with a more civilizing effect on its surroundings.

The buildings are variations of two basic designs, which are arranged in the pattern a-b-a-a-a-b-a-a-a-b-a-a-a-b. Each of the two designs is in the classic split-level configuration, which allows separate access to the basement. The materials palette is simple but impeccably chosen: brick in three colors, accents of copper and cast stone, and terra cotta at the basement level. Sumptuous landscaping is integrated into the streetscape, and each townhouse has an enclosed rear garden. The apartments, some of which include terraces visible from the street, are generously daylit.

A C G to Hoyt-Schermerhorn

73

377 Pacific Street
377 Pacific Street (at Bond St.)
Clay Miller, Bergen Street Studio
2005

This adaptive reuse project transformed a 1930s garage into an elegant two-family townhouse. The owner, Marc Appelbaum of Radius Construction Group, originally planned to tear down the existing building and start anew. The design architect, who was sufficiently inspired by the garage's aesthetic possibilities, eventually persuaded the owner to retain it. Originally trained as an architect, the owner contributed to the project's design and also performed construction.

The designers successfully navigated the conservative design aesthetic prevalent in the Boerum Hill neighborhood, much of which is an historic district. The new upper floors exude a bright, contemporary feel. They feature horizontal wood screening, which imparts quiet warmth and blends the addition to the garage and adjacent nineteenth-century houses. The lower unit is essentially on one level below grade, but includes a double-height living area which "pops up" in the middle of the building. The upper unit is a triplex.

A C G to Hoyt-Schermerhorn

74

L3 Condominiums
191-193 Luquer Street (at Court St.)
Office 606 Design + Construction
2007

This project skillfully integrates the former St. Mary's convent with two new buildings, which flank the old building on each side and are mirror images of each other. The architects decided to set the new buildings back from the streetwall in order to create ornamental front yards and to set off the existing building. (See Number 3 for another residential addition to a nineteenth-century building; see Number 5 for a project with a similar relationship to its street.) The original entrance in the existing building has been removed and infilled, and a new entrance has been provided in each of the two new buildings.

The additions are skillfully proportioned so as to complement the existing building. Although they are rendered largely in steel and glass, they include brick accents which allude to the old masonry facade. Steel is painted gray and is elegantly detailed. The project includes twelve new condominiums.

 G to Smith-9th Sts.

75

Hillside Mausoleum
Tranquility Gardens
500 25th Street (at Fifth Ave.)
Platt Byard Dovell White Architects LLP
2005/2007

These twin projects, by the same architect and for the same client, are located in Green-Wood Cemetery, which was founded in 1838 and is probably the best-known cemetery in New York. Green-Wood's vast size (478 acres) and bucolic landscape architecture subsequently became a model for Central and Prospect Parks as well as for suburban development. The mausoleum and columbarium share the same spirit of restful tranquility intended by the designers of the cemetery, but have a contemporary architectural vocabulary suffused with the influence of Eastern design philosophy.

The projects exhibit exemplary use of natural materials, water features, and daylighting. Elements common to both include a simple but sumptuous materials palette of Brazilian hardwood, granite, and steel, as well as pyramidal forms which serve as skylights. Built into a steep hillside, the mausoleum offers street access from the lowest level and access to the hilltop from the roof deck. The columbarium consists of three pavilions set in a semicircle, which are connected to one another by walkways and by a pool filled with koi fish.

 to 25th St.

76

David Salle Artist Residence and Studio
81 Hanson Place (at S. Portland Ave.)
Christian Hubert Studio
David Fratianne Architect, PLLC
2005

The artist for whom this project was designed was born in Norman, Oklahoma, but has lived in New York since completing his studies at the California Institute of the Arts in the early 1970s. The designers' intent was to create distinct spaces for work and for living while at the same time providing a "seamless interior flow" between them. The project is actually a renovation and combining of two existing nineteenth century buildings, which consisted of a 2-story brick schoolhouse and a four-story townhouse.

In the final design, the schoolhouse has become the studio, while the townhouse has become the residence. The envelope has been enlarged by the addition of a cantilevered façade: clad in stucco and standing seam zinc panels, it projects over the sidewalk at the second, third and four floors. Private exterior space was provided by inserting a roof terrace at the third floor level between the two structures, and by adding additional balconies to the loft space on the fourth floor.

B Q 2 3 4 5 to Atlantic Ave.
C to Lafayette Ave.

77

Fort Greene Townhouse
208 Vanderbilt Avenue (at Willoughby Ave.)
David Hotson Architect
Adjaye Associates
2006

Architecturally, this is one of the most innovative townhouses to be constructed in New York in recent memory. Its most striking feature is its cladding, which consists of polycarbonate panels with a variegated monochrome pattern. The edges of the panels butt together, creating a smooth, neutral-colored surface; this is maintained by the flush-mounted, dark tinted street windows. A dramatic contrast is provided by the rear façade, which presents an all-glass face to the enclosed garden behind the building.

Although belied by its cutting-edge architecture, the townhouse is actually a reconstructed industrial building. It houses two duplex studios, each of which provides a workspace for an artist.

G to Clinton-Washington Aves

78

Vincent J. Stabile Student Residence Hall
200 Willoughby Ave. (at Grand St.)
Pasanella + Klein, Stolzman + Berg
Architects, PC
1999

The architects won this project, which includes an art school as well as a dormitory, through an invited design competition. It is noteworthy for its innovative configuration of residential spaces and for integrating them with an art studio and gallery. The architects successfully responded to a limited budget and a somewhat unusual program with a simple but effective materials palette and a layout which provides effective circulation both inside and outside the building.

The building's basic configuration consists of three blocks of residential units arranged along a spine, with the art gallery and studio to the south. Realizing that in art school "homework is design," the architects inserted design studios into the residential floors of the building. In order to do away with the floor-to-floor isolation common in dorms, conventional "student lounges" were eschewed and double-height common spaces were introduced. The undergraduate dorm houses 240 students in four-person suites, each consisting of two double rooms with a shared bath.

G to Classon Ave.

79

Juliana Curran Terian Design Center
200 Willoughby Ave. (at Grand St.)
hanrahanMeyers Architects
2007

This project is an infill between the existing Steuben Hall and Pratt Studios. Clad in hand-finished stainless steel panels, the building provides an elegant contrast with its traditional masonry neighbors. The front façade, which cantilevers over the entry, faces north in order to provide consistent natural lighting to the interior throughout the day. A new circulation bridge to the south overlooks a new courtyard, which serves as an "outdoor room" for informal meetings.

The double-height main space is principally used for receptions and for the exhibition of artwork. Screens are provided for rear projection so that slides or videos may be displayed to the quadrangle. Alternatively, the interior of the building may be fully darkened during daylight hours in order to present slides or videos in the interior.

G to Classon Ave.

80

Higgins Hall
61 St. James Place (at Lafayette Ave.)
Steven Holl Architects
Rogers Marvel Architects, PLLC
2005

Like the Terian Design Center (Number 79), Higgins Hall is an infill between two existing buildings, and provides a single new main entry serving both. The project was initiated after the existing nineteenth-century buildings were severely damaged in a 1996 fire. The program includes a gallery, studios, auditorium, digital resource center, review room, and workshops.

In dramatic contrast to the flanking masonry buildings, the exterior of the addition is clad in a system of insulated, structural glass planks. Despite its novelty, this is a relatively inexpensive material, and has the added advantage of giving the building a warm glow at night. The façade also features a carefully composed, asymmetrical pattern of operable fenestration, which offers glimpses of the interior as well as of the courtyard beyond. A single sawtooth skylight provides north light to the interior. Salvaged bricks from the destroyed portions of the old buildings were reused to construct the new plaza.

G to Classon Ave.

81

PrattStore
550 Myrtle Avenue (at Emerson Pl.)
Richard Scherr
2005

This new bookstore for Pratt Institute is intended to serve the public at large as well as Pratt students. It was designed by the school's Director of Facilities Planning, who is also an adjunct architecture professor. In order to keep costs down, the design made extensive use of prefabricated components by Butler Building Systems. As befits a store serving design students, the finished building conveys energy and youthfulness.

The exterior is inexpensively clad in white metal panels and is enlivened by graphics and decorative banners. Exposed steel members are painted gray and red to provide additional contrast. The major feature is the entry, where a corner has been subtracted from the rectilinear mass; a steel tube canopy denotes the entrance and provides a visual pull to the interior. Exposed exterior structural elements are repeated inside, and clerestory lighting creates a largely daylit space.

G to Classon Ave.

82

On Prospect Park
Grand Army Plaza
Richard Meier & Partners
2008

This project is a follow-up to Meier's three apartment buildings in Greenwich Village (Number 22). It embodies a design aesthetic similar to that of the earlier buildings, albeit transposed to a larger site and more dignified, Old World surroundings.

The building is fifteen stories in height and contains 102 apartments, nearly all of which have balconies. There are eight different rooftop gardens, one of which is open to all tenants. The base is articulated to match the street scale of the neighborhood, while the tower is massed and scaled in a grandiose manner appropriate to its prominent site adjacent to Grand Army Plaza and Prospect Park.

 to Grand Army Plaza

83

Poly Prep Lower School
50 Prospect Park West (at First St.)
Platt Byard Dovell White Architects LLP
2008

This project is an addition to, and renovation of, an 1892 mansion which was originally constructed as a two-family home for Henry Hulbert and his married daughter. Designed by Montrose W. Morris in the Romanesque Revival style, the building has served as an educational facility since the 1920s (its initial such occupant was the Ethical Culture School, followed by the Woodward Park School). The present owner purchased the building in the late 1990s.

The addition provides eight classrooms, a multi-purpose room, and a dance studio, as well as a new building entrance. Work included renovating the original building, reorganizing its interiors to meet new program requirements, and rationalizing its vertical circulation elements (particularly the main stair). The design does not copy adjacent exterior materials (glass and limestone are used rather than brick and brownstone masonry) but complements neighboring Park Slope buildings by evoking their compositional asymmetry, sculptural quality, and relationship to the street. It achieves further harmony with its neighbors through impeccable detailing, skillful proportioning and deft color choices.

to Grand Army Plaza

84

Brooklyn Museum
Entry Pavilion and Plaza
200 Eastern Parkway (at Washington Ave.)
Polshek Partnership Architects LLP
2004

This was a brilliant solution to a difficult problem. The original McKim, Mead and White building, built between 1893 and 1915 (and never fully realized), included a monumental entry stair rising a full floor to the lobby on the second level. A 1935 WPA renovation, which removed the stair, made entry less physically strenuous but dramatically altered the building's appearance. Renewed interest in the museum in the 1980s led to a master plan competition, won by Polshek Partnership in association with Arata Isosaki. This project is one step in realizing the new master plan.

Rather than simply recreate the original stairs, which would have created access problems, the architects designed a new pavilion which incorporates entry at grade. The masterful composition includes amphitheater-like stairs to the south, a sculpted stair to the north, a steel-and-glass canopy which complements the museum's colonnaded façade, and a landscaped plaza with a delightful water feature. The project seamlessly integrates interior and exterior spaces and provides a new outdoor space for leisure and performances.

to Eastern Parkway-
Brooklyn Museum

85

Brooklyn Children's Museum
145 Brooklyn Avenue (at St. Mark's Ave.)
Rafael Viñoly Architects
2008

The Brooklyn Children's Museum, the world's first, was founded in 1899 and moved into its present building, designed by Hardy Holzman Pfeiffer Associates, in 1977. The two-story Viñoly addition doubles existing space and includes exhibition galleries, a café, library, classrooms, offices, and a rooftop terrace. The L-shaped building is intended to integrate with adjacent Brower Park and to have an engaging, welcoming street presence.

At the entrance, full height glazing invites visitors into the bright, daylit lobby. The remainder of the orthogonal first floor is clad in green and orange metal panels (with elegant architectural lettering). Overhead cantilevers the billowy, bright yellow second story, which is sheathed in over eight million yellow glazed 1" x 1" ceramic tiles set diagonally (in 16" x 16" sheets). The form is pockmarked with round windows reminiscent of portholes, which are placed in a whimsical, seemingly random fashion.

C to Kingston-Throop Aves.
3 to Kingston Ave.

86

Brooklyn Jewish Children's Museum
792 Eastern Parkway (at Kingston Ave.)
Gwathmey Siegel & Associates Architects LLC
2004

The Brooklyn Jewish Children's Museum is billed as the first museum of its kind in the world. The idea was born with an international not-for-profit children's organization, Tzivos Hashem, which beginning in 1986 held an annual Jewish Children's Expo at the Jacob Javits Convention Center. The current building proves that Brooklyn, which invented children's museums more than 100 years ago, still has a flair for constructing them.

In comparison with its nearby secular neighbor (Number 85), this building conveys augmented seriousness of purpose. The two streetwalls create visual interest by incorporating a wide variety of materials and forms. (The building's location in a residential neighborhood created an imperative to render its large facades in an appropriately small scale.) Site-designed artwork has been integrated extremely successfully into both the front elevation and the entry plaza. Douglas/Gallagher and Nash Brookes designed the exhibits, which emphasize interactive multimedia. In addition to the exhibition galleries, program spaces include a cafeteria, gift shop, event spaces, and administrative offices.

3 to Kingston Ave.

87

Local Union 580
Ornamental & Architectural Ironworkers
Apprentice Training Facility
37-31 30th St (at 38th Ave.)
Daniel Goldner Architects
2004

This adaptive reuse of a former warehouse and auto body shop is all about layering. The client's primary objectives were to showcase the skills of union ironworkers and to inspire the apprentices enrolled in the union's three-year training program. To these ends, the bland masonry façade has been enveloped in a tour de force of architectural metalwork.

At street level, painted aluminum panels in a regular pattern are interrupted at unexpected points by slotted windows, doors, and even a roll-up door in a wall screening the adjacent parking lot. The sumptuous entryway includes a steel canopy with elegant architectural lettering, stainless steel panels, colored glass, and etched brass. Above the first floor, the brick wall is screened with stainless steel mesh. An irregular, articulated horizontal gap at the second floor level reveals a bit of the brick and accentuates the change in materials.

 to 39th Ave.

88

Korean Presbyterian Church of New York
43-05 37th Avenue (at 43rd St.)
Greg Lynn, FORM
Garofolo Architects
Michael McInturf Architects
1999

This Korean megachurch, designed by one of California's most cutting-edge architects, is actually an adaptive reuse project. The building occupies the former Knickerbocker Laundry Company (later Naarde-UOP Fragrances), a factory building dating to 1932 which had been vacant for decades. Although many of the period Streamline Moderne forms are clearly visible, the form and character of the building have been dramatically altered.

The exterior is largely rectilinear, with the dramatic exception of the steel structure enclosing the exterior egress stairs which serve the main sanctuary: clad in metal panels, it forms a dynamic series of nested polygons. At the interior, these forms are reiterated in the design of the sanctuary as well as in that of the smaller assembly spaces. At the exterior, new and old forms are articulated with Kalwall and anodized storefront. A steel screen over the former main entrance to the factory, which directly faces the nearby Long Island Railroad, appropriately features a quotation from Lamentations 1:12.

R V G to Steinway St.

89

New York Hall of Science addition
47-01 111th Street (at 47th Ave.)
Polshek Partnership Architects LLP
2004

This is the most recent expansion to the New York Hall of Science, which occupies a building originally designed by Harrison and Abramovitz for the 1964 World's Fair. Dubbed "The Cathedral of Science," the original building, while awe-inspiring, proved too cramped and inflexible for a growing museum. In 1996 Polshek Partnership completed a sturdy addition, which pragmatically contributed a new entrance, cafeteria, and science playground.

The present project, again by Polshek, provides additional space for exhibitions, exhibition preparation, and shop facilities. The main feature is the "Hall of Light," a daylit steel truss and Kalwall structure with a translucent, horizontal form (contrasting effectively with the original building's opaque verticality). James Carpenter contributed an elegant sculpture at the west end of the building. The project is welcome proof that Polshek can design museum spaces on a limited budget (see Numbers 63 and 84 for more sumptuous Polshek commissions). Adjacent to the addition, a new landscaped area accommodates the early Space Age attractions of the renovated Rocket Park.

 to 111th St.

90

Queens Theatre in the Park expansion
Flushing Meadows Corona Park
Caples Jefferson Architects
Lee/Timchula Architects
2008

The low, circular building which houses the Queens Theatre in the Park was originally built for the 1964 World's Fair as an auxiliary structure to Philip Johnson's New York State Pavilion. Following its two-year Fair run showcasing a cycloramic production, the building was converted to a theatre (in 1972) and was used by various organizations until 1985. The present user formed in 1989 and in 1993 reopened the renovated building, which by then included a 464-seat main stage theatre and a 99-seat studio theatre. The current expansion has added a 75-seat cabaret performance space, a full service cafe; and a new lobby/reception area.

The architecture skillfully evokes the pop Jet Age aesthetic exemplified by the World's Fair Pavilion (which was memorably featured in *Men in Black*). The reception area's deep orange "nebula ceiling," which includes an oculus, is especially dramatic at night, when it appears to hover luminously. Materials include polished brass, terrazzo, an elegant storefront system, and stainless steel mesh wrapped around the exterior.

7 to Mets-Willets Point

91

Aquatic Center and Ice Rink
Flushing Meadows Corona Park
Handel Architects, LLP
Kevin Hom & Andrew Goldman Architects, PC
2008

This is the largest recreation complex ever constructed in a New York City park, and the first indoor public pool built in the city in four decades. Although initial plans called for only an intermediate size pool, visions of a 2012 NYC Olympics resulted in an upgrade to an Olympic-size pool and the addition of an NHL-regulation ice rink. These elements are arranged linearly, with the entryway and lobby space located between. The pool area is extensively daylit, and the inviting double-height lobby is sheathed in glass.

The building, situated on the edge of Flushing Meadows Corona Park, serves as a metaphorical bridge between the adjacent neighborhood and the green expanses of the park. The sinuous, cable-stayed structure, in a configuration typically used for literal bridges, therefore seems an apt design solution for the support of the building's roof. Like the nearby New York State Pavilion and Unisphere, which were built for the 1964 World's Fair, the building has a dramatic profile and is clearly visible from the adjacent expressway.

 to Mets-Willets Point

92

Queens Botanical Garden
Visitor and Administration Center
43-50 Main Street (at Dahlia Ave.)
BKSK Architects LLP
2008

This spectacular project was designed to showcase environmental design. It consists of three major components: a forecourt and freestanding roof canopy, supported on eight columns; a reception and administration building, and a below-ground auditorium space with a green roof.

The project masterfully blends architecture and landscaping and is particularly notable for water management: a 24,000 gallon cistern collects rainwater from the freestanding canopy and stores it for later use in the fountain and water channels. Other features include recycled and renewable materials, photovoltaic panels, a geothermal heat exchange system, and graywater/stormwater management systems. The majority of the interior spaces are daylit.

7 to Flushing-Main Street

93

Flushing Branch Library
41-17 Main Street (at 41st Ave. and Kissena Blvd.)
Polshek Partnership Architects LLP
2000

The Queens Library is the largest public library system in the United States in terms of circulation, and this building is its largest branch. This meant that the architects were faced with complex programmatic requirements, which included an auditorium, multi-purpose room, conference rooms, exhibition areas, an Adult Learning Center, and an International Resource Center. An additional challenge was the difficult triangular site at an extremely busy intersection, located in the heart of downtown Flushing.

The resulting building resembles the prow of a ship. At the point of the triangle is a landscaped entry plaza whose granite steps feature tributes to various literary figures. Sheathed in glass curtain wall, the Main Street façade features a sumptuous etched glass installation by Yong Soon Min. The more sedate Kissena Boulevard façade is treated with granite in various finishes. The building and exterior spaces have become focal points of the community, as evidenced by the fact that they teem with throngs of people each day of the week.

7 to Flushing-Main Street

94

High School for Construction Trades, Engineering and Architecture
94-06 104th Street (at 94th Ave.)
STV Incorporated
2006

The mission of the HSCTEA, which is focused on the design and construction industry, is to prepare its 925+ students for college, technical school, and post-graduation apprenticeships. To this end, a primary goal of the building's design was to present a strong architectural statement which would serve as a teaching tool. Accordingly, it exhibits a variety of architectural materials, workmanlike detailing, and exposed mechanical and electrical systems. The front elevation alone presents cast-in-place structural concrete, precast concrete panels, metal panels, brick masonry, punched aluminum windows, glass block, and glass curtain wall.

Building facilities include specialized laboratories for computer aided design and drafting (CADD), mechanical drafting, model building, and construction technology. The interiors of the building are largely daylit, and public art is prominently displayed.

  to 104th St.

95

LIRR Jamaica Station Intermodal Facility
Sutphin Boulevard and Archer Avenue
Port Authority of New York and New Jersey
2003

This building is the most spectacular portion of the much-anticipated AirTrain project, a ten-mile light rail system which now connects John F. Kennedy International Airport to New York's passenger rail infrastructure. The facility connects three rail stations: the new AirTrain station, the Long Island Rail Road (LIRR) Jamaica Station, and the New York City Transit (NYCT) Sutphin Boulevard/ Archer Avenue station. Design work was performed in-house by the Port Authority, with the assistance of numerous design and engineering firms.

The focal point of the complex is the dramatic seven-story Vertical Circulation Building/Central Control Building. (Complementing its glassed atrium are outsized wall graphics of a piano keyboard and a long list of musicians' names which honors the history of jazz in Queens.) Even more impressive are the sweeping (and massive) steel truss canopies which span the LIRR platforms. The project also provided handsome new signage and graphics throughout the complex. Escalators and elevators permit smooth connections without negotiating stairs, a welcome respite for luggage-toting air passengers.

E J Z to Sutphin Blvd.

96

Terminal 4
John F. Kennedy International Airport
Skidmore, Owings and Merrill LLP
2001

In 1996, SOM was asked to design a replacement for their 1957 International Arrivals Building, which had been rendered obsolete by dramatically increased air travel volume as well as by increasingly stringent security requirements. The new terminal is designed to handle 3,200 passengers per hour (seven million a year), and was envisioned as part of a larger airport reconstruction which will eventually replace all nine original terminals. The new AirTrain, which connects the terminals with each other and with two subway stations, glides futuristically into the center of the building (granted, Disney World did it twenty years earlier). The project is configured on three levels: arrivals concourse at ground level, retail and food court above, departures hall at the top.

The building's most noteworthy feature is its dramatic roof. Designed as a sweeping, fluid form, it is supported by a spectacular triangulated truss system. Extensive glazing (skylights and curtain walls) gives the building a remarkable feeling of openness. The interior is extensively graced with artwork, including a restored Alexander Calder mobile ("Flight") salvaged from the demolished 1957 terminal. At this writing, the terminal is served by forty-six airlines.

A to Howard Beach, then AirTrain
E J Z to Sutphin Blvd., then AirTrain

97

South Bronx Classic Community Center, at Melrose House

286 East 156th Street (at Concourse Village E.)
Agrest & Gandelsonas Architects
Wank Adams Slavin Associates, Inc.
2001

An interesting recent project type is the community center for the existing public housing complex. The NYC Department of Housing has demonstrated a willingness to experiment with different architectural styles (albeit with limited budgets) and has generated some interesting results. (Examples include 465 St. Ann's Avenue and 625 Castle Hill Avenue, both in The Bronx; and 34-30 137th Street, Queens.)

For this project, a primary design goal was to achieve openness and a welcoming persona, and to avoid the fortresslike appearance of many public housing structures. To that end, functions are articulated with a simple geometric massing and a tripartite color scheme. The composition consists of an oval form, sheathed in metal panels, which contains the gymnasium; a curtain-walled modified rectangle which houses classrooms, studios and community spaces; and a link between the two forms which contains the main entrance. (The three forms are colored gray, white and red.) The architects played up a solid-void contrast by using curtain wall juxtaposed with unfenestrated cladding. Graphics include neon signage and architectural lettering.

to 3rd Ave.-149th St.

98

Bronx Museum of the Arts addition
1040 Grand Concourse (at 165th St.)
Arquitectonica Architects
2006

The Young Israel Synagogue, which was completed in 1961, was later capably converted into the Bronx Museum, which has occupied the building since 1982. The current project is the first phase of a master plan which is intended to eventually replace the existing museum building. The ambitious second phase of the project will create a 189-unit residential co-op.

The modestly sized but assertive addition conveys a jaunty, engaging presence, with a dramatic folded façade. Tucked into the creases, the fritted glass windows begin to break down the barrier between inside and outside, and to engage the street. The metal panels which clad the building have unusual diagonal joints. The lobby adjoins a tiny but bright gift shop as well as a leisurely ramp which accesses a new gallery. Other program areas include event spaces, an outdoor terrace, and a classroom level. Articulated brick walls mark locations intended for future expansion.

 to 167th St.

99

Bronx YMCA Aquatics and Fitness Center
2 Castle Hill Avenue (at Zerega Ave.)
Donald Blair & Partners Architects, LLP
2006

Occupying a suburban site at the end of a cul-de-sac, this building is primarily visible only from the front. It enjoys assured, articulate massing and a quiet neutral color scheme of whites and grays. Located close to the water and to Castle Hill Park, this building subtly but unmistakably evokes a nautical theme, appropriate as well given its function. The pool and recreational facilities allowed the expansion of programs previously confined to the adjacent YMCA Howard & Minerva Munch Day Camp and Family Center.

The simple but effective palette of inexpensive materials consists of Kalwall, ground faced concrete block, white metal paneling with horizontal ribs, anodized aluminum fenestration, and exposed structural steel painted battleship gray. The steel members and connections are attractively designed and are exposed inside and out, which enables the highlighting of features such as crossbracing. The building's configuration clearly expresses its various interior functions as well as its entrance, and its identity is unmistakably conveyed through the artful use of the familiar YMCA logo.

100

Iglesia Evangelica de Co-op City Metodista Unida
2350 Palmer Avenue (at Huchinson River Parkway E.)
Gluckman Mayner Architects
2005

This is, without a doubt, the brightest, crispest church in New York, and is proof that Modernist design can be quite happily realized on a modest budget. The simple but dynamic L-shaped building accommodates a narthex, sanctuary, chapel, large meeting room, and support spaces. Located on a cramped site in a flood plain, the building is sensibly raised on columns. This creates parking for twenty-three cars underneath the building and allows the segregation of vehicular and pedestrian entrances.

The congregation, which had worshiped in a basement for years, was passionately interested in creating bright, daylit spaces. The architects achieved this through generous corridor fenestration and judiciously placed clerestory lighting. On the building's exterior, imaging is skillfully—and unmistakably—achieved through the use of a steel steeple and a United Methodist Church logo at each end of the building. The entire project truly exhibits a great deal of panache and flair.

6 to Pelham Bay Park

101

Leon Levy Visitor Center
New York Botanical Garden
H3 Hardy Collaboration Architecture, LLP
2004

This project was planned to create an elegant transition between its urban surroundings and the pastoral garden, and to showcase the mature trees and natural topography of the surrounding Arthur and Janet Ross Conifer Arboretum. In laying out the design, careful attention was paid to paths of travel and the framing of views. Extensive areas of glass give the Center an airy, tranquil feel.

The quiet composition consists of four buildings arranged around an axial path, which is terminated at one end by the garden entry and at the other by a water feature. At the entry, an open pavilion includes a steel reinterpretation of a colonnaded trellis. The buildings utilize a contemporary materials palette which emphasizes structural honesty and natural materials. Roofs are formed of curved laminated wood beams, which are supported on an elegant system of steel pipe columns and stainless steel crossbracing. Spaces below are infilled with varying combinations of partial-height bluestone walls, clerestory windows, floor-to-ceiling aluminum curtain wall, and elegant gray metal panels.

B D to Bedford Park Blvd.

A

Street Furniture
Grimshaw Architects LLP
2006

In July 2005, after an extensive competitive bidding process, the New York City Department of Transportation (NYCDOT) awarded a 20-year contract to Spain-based Cemusa (pronounced say-moo-sa) for the design, manufacture, installation and maintenance of new street furniture throughout the five boroughs. The work is to be done at no cost to the city, with the advertising revenue to cover Cemusa's expenses. The new street furniture, which includes bus shelters, bike shelters, newsstands, and automatic public toilets (APTs), is made primarily of stainless steel and laminated tempered glass.

The pragmatic, stylish family of designs was developed in concert with the NYCDOT and the Department of Consumer Affairs. Bus shelters display the name of the stop in illuminated letters and include lighting as well as optional benches. (Cemusa plans to install 3,300 such bus shelters by 2011.) Bike shelters are a modification of the bus shelter design. Newsstands include lighting, shelving, storage and electrical outlets. APTs are accessible and air conditioned, and have an automatic system which cleans and disinfects the toilet bowl and floor after each use.

B

Taxi Logo
Claudia Christen, Smart Design
2007

This makeover is the first phase in an ambitious project which will completely transform New York City's taxis. (Future phase-ins include an all-hybrid fleet by 2012 and innovative interior seating plans which will accommodate wheelchair users.) The design of the first visual revision since 1970 of the iconic "yellow cab" required close collaboration with the New York City Taxi and Limousine Commission. In the course of developing twenty-five draft designs, the team studied archival material (including Hollywood films) and examined the graphics of other taxi fleets from around the world.

In the end, the main graphic was the result of a compromise, reached by combining the city's existing "NYC" logo (used by NYC & Company, New York's marketing organization) with the "TAXI" developed by the design team (a custom font intended to evoke "the cab of the future.") On the rear door, a fare panel includes an icon of a passenger hailing a cab. The medallion registration number on the rear fender is enhanced by a checkered stream of rectangles, inspired by the much-beloved Checker cab common at mid-century.

Lower Manhattan Map

Financial District
TriBeCa
SoHo
Lower East Side
East Village
Greenwich Village

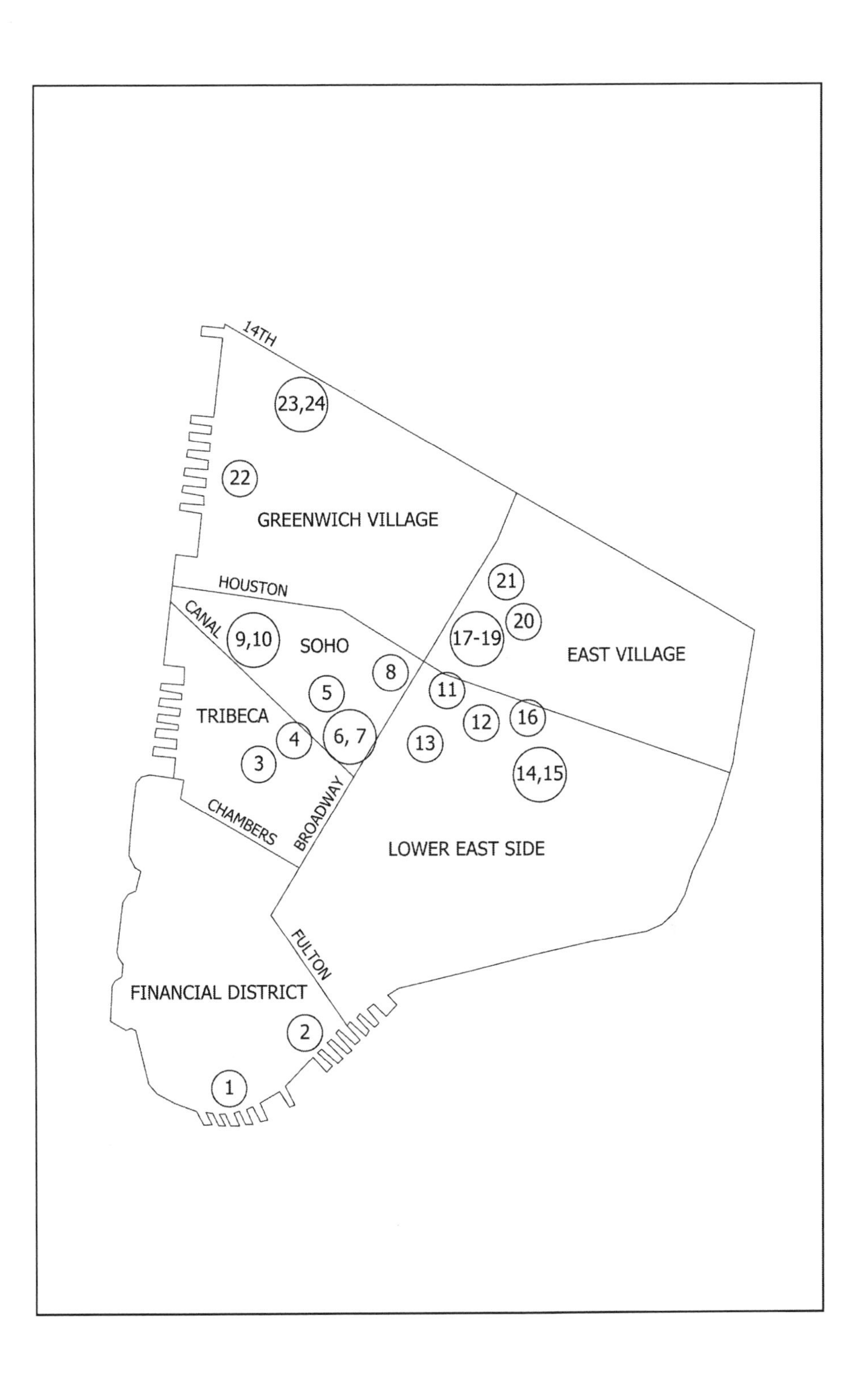
14TH
23,24
22
GREENWICH VILLAGE
HOUSTON
CANAL
9,10
SOHO
21
20
17-19
EAST VILLAGE
8
5
11
TRIBECA
4
6, 7
12
16
3
13
14,15
CHAMBERS
BROADWAY
LOWER EAST SIDE
FULTON
FINANCIAL DISTRICT
2
1

Mid-Manhattan Map

Chelsea
Gramercy Park
Murray Hill
Midtown
Times Square/Columbus Circle
West Side

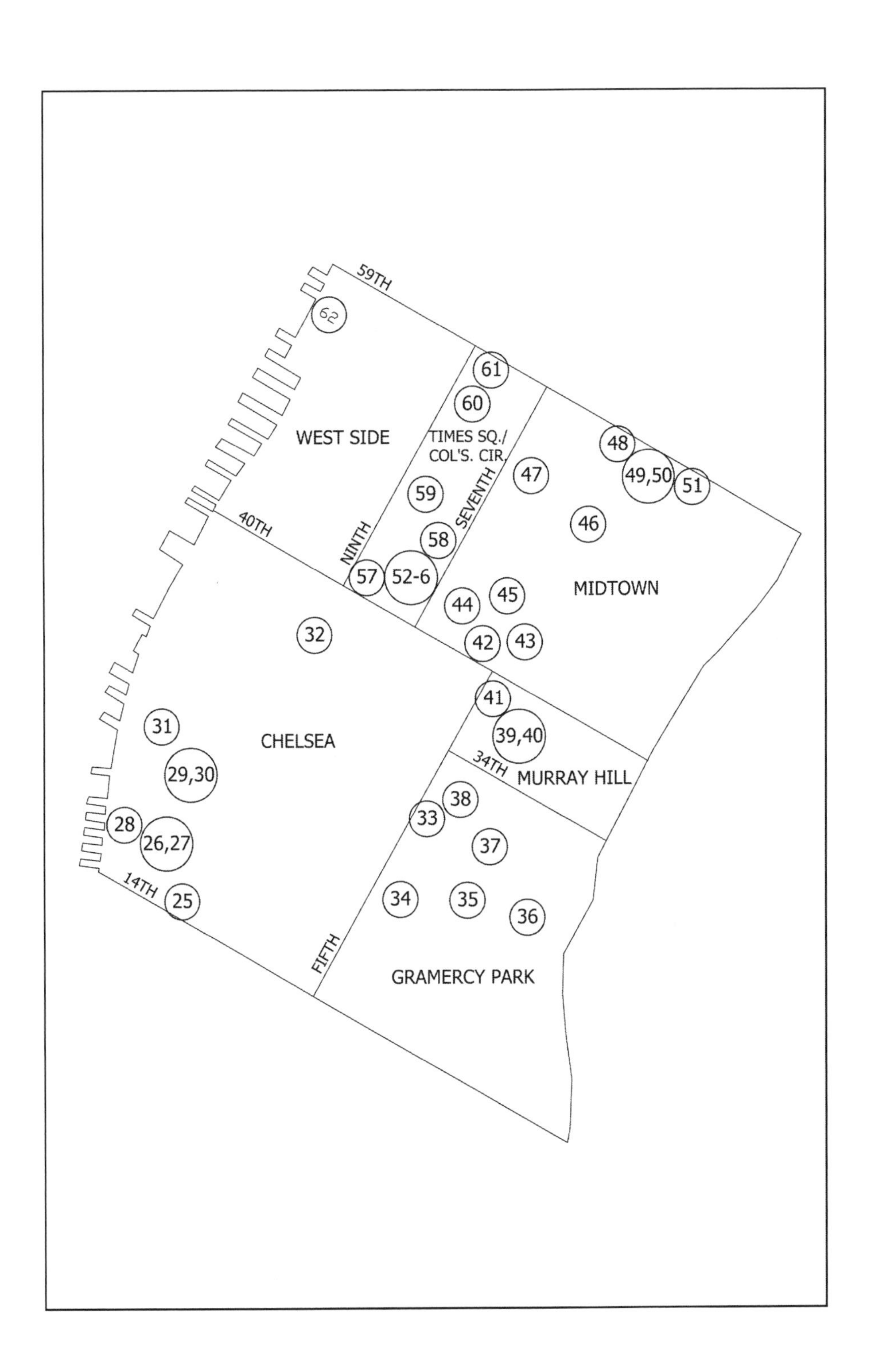
59TH
62
61
60
WEST SIDE
TIMES SQ./
COL'S. CIR.
48
49,50
51
47
59
SEVENTH
46
40TH
58
NINTH
57
52-6
MIDTOWN
45
44
32
42
43
41
31
CHELSEA
39,40
34TH
MURRAY HILL
29,30
38
33
28
26,27
37
14TH
25
34
35
36
FIFTH
GRAMERCY PARK

Upper Manhattan Map

Upper West Side
Harlem
Upper East Side

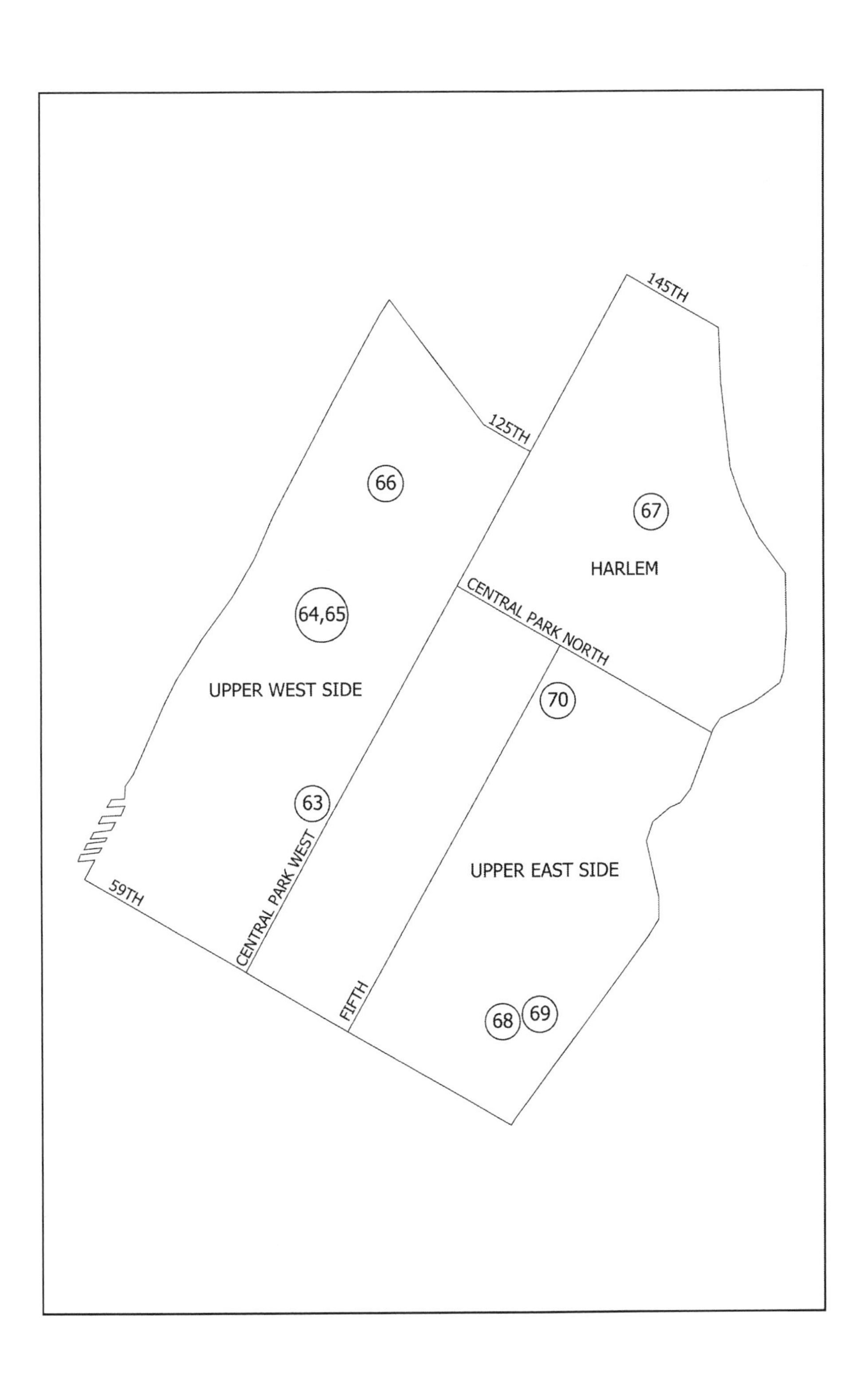
145TH
125TH
66
67
HARLEM
CENTRAL PARK NORTH
64,65
UPPER WEST SIDE
70
63
CENTRAL PARK WEST
UPPER EAST SIDE
59TH
FIFTH
68
69

Brooklyn Map

71
72
77
78-81
73
76
85
74
82
83
86
84
75

Queens Map

87
88
89
91
90
92
93
95
94
96

The Bronx Map

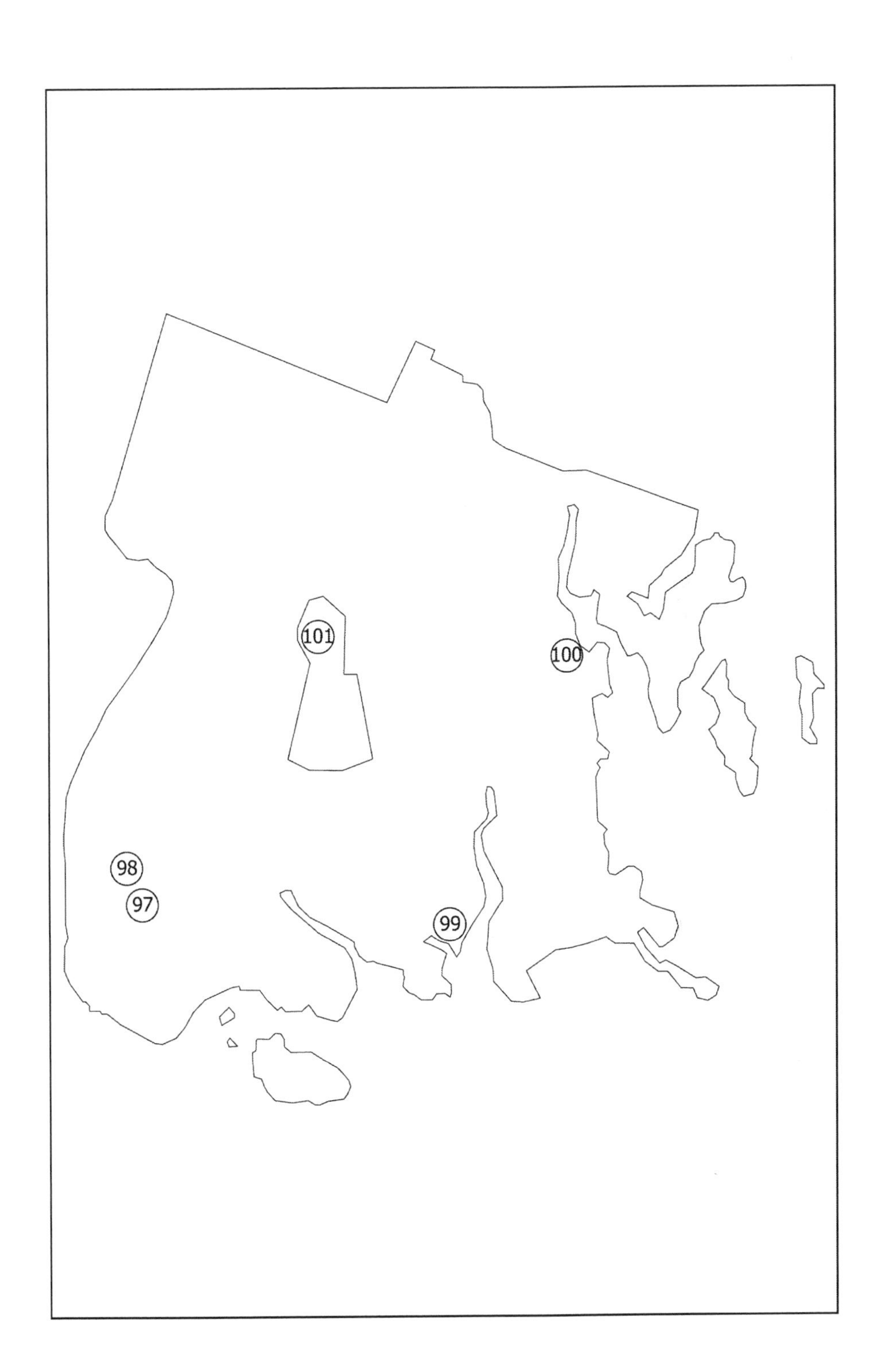
101
100
98
97
99

Geographic Index

27	Four Five Nine	Della Valle Bernheimer
28	The IAC Building	Frank Gehry
29	Jim Kempner Fine Art	Smith and Thompson Architects
30	High Line 519	Lindy Roy, Roy Co.
31	Chelsea Arts Tower	Kossar & Garry Architects Gluckman Mayner Architects HOK
32	37 Arts - Baryshnikov Arts Center	Averitt Associates Landy Verderame Arianna Architects TEKArchitects

Gramercy Park

33	Sky House	FXFowle Architects, PC
34	One Madison Park	Cetra/Ruddy Incorporated
35	Baruch College	Kohn Pederson Fox Associates
36	New York City Office of the Chief Medical Examiner (OCME) DNA Forensics Biology Laboratory	Perkins Eastman
37	Gramercy 145	Manuel Glas
38	M127	SHoP Architects PC

Murray Hill

39	The Morgan Library & Museum addition	Renzo Piano Building Workshop Beyer Blinder Belle Architects & Planners
40	Scandinavia House	Polshek Partnership Architects LLP
41	425 Fifth Avenue	Michael Graves & Associates H. Thomas O'Hara Architect, PLLC

Midtown

42	New York Public Library Humanities and Social Sciences Library South Court	Davis Brody Bond
43	505 Fifth Avenue	Kohn Pederson Fox Associates
44	Bank of America Tower	Cook + Fox Architects Gensler
45	Harvard Club of New York City	Davis Brody Bond
46	Austrian Cultural Forum	Raimund Abraham
47	American Folk Art Museum	Tod Williams Billie Tsien + Associates
48	Apple Store Fifth Avenue	Bohlin Cywinski Jackson Moed de Armas & Shannon, Architects
49	LVMH Tower	Christian de Portzamparc The Hillier Group
50	59E59 Theaters	Leo Modrcin, uRED Architecture Franke, Gottsegen, Cox Architects
51	The Bloomberg Tower/One Beacon Court	Cesar Pelli & Associates

Times Square

52	The Reuters Building	Fox & Fowle Architects PC
53	Condé Nast Building	Fox & Fowle Architects PC
54	Ernst & Young	Kohn Pederson Fox Associates
55	The Times Square Tower	Skidmore, Owings and Merrill LLP
56	The New 42nd Street Studios	Platt Byard Dovell White Architects LLP

Queens

The Bronx

Honorable Mention

Alphabetical Index

Index by Architect

Made in the USA
San Bernardino, CA
19 December 2013